WORSHIP-CENTERED YOUTH MINISTRY

WORSHIP-CENTERED YOUTH MINISTRY

A COMPASS FOR GUIDING YOUTH INTO GOD'S STORY

by

JON MIDDENDORF

Beacon Hill Press of Kansas City
and

WordAction Publishing Company™
Kansas City, Missouri

Editor: James K. Hampton
Assistant Editor: Jeff Edmondson

Copyright 2000
by Beacon Hill Press of Kansas City

ISBN 083-411-8262

Printed in the
United States of America

Library of Congress Cataloging-in-Publication Data

Middendorf, Jon.
    Worship-centered youth ministry : a compass for guiding youth into God's story / by Jon Midden-
dorf.
        p. cm.
    Includes bibliographical references.
    ISBN 0-8341-1826-2
    1. Church work with youth—Church of the Nazarene. 2. People of God. I. Title.
BV4447 .M494 2000
259'.23—dc21

                                                                            00-049817

10   9   8   7   6   5   4   3   2   1

I dedicate this book to . . .

Dave Curtiss—your vision and foresight in establishing the TEAM NYI Training Program led to the formation of the seminar on which this book is based;

The TEAM NYI Trainers—iron sharpens iron, and none of what has been done could have been done without all of you: James Amos, Don Bergland, Gary Hartke, Mark Holcombe, Monty Stewart, Ron Jackson, Buddy Marston, Beverly Cook, Tim Milburn, and Pat Wiens;

The Oklahoma City First family—for being family to my family for the past decade, especially all of you who have survived my ministry to teens over the years;

My parents and my brother and sister—for your belief in me;

My wife and my partner, Kelly—who continues to teach me about love and faith;

My daughter, Taylor—who inspires me toward growth and consistency;

My editor, Jim Hampton—for keeping me focused and for helping to sharpen, synthesize, and organize what has many times been a pile of unorganized thoughts. I appreciate your heart and friendship.

"We belong to one another only through and in Jesus Christ."
—Dietrich Bonhoeffer, *Life Together*

Contents

Preface

I am one of you. Whether you are a professional or volunteer youth worker, a Sunday School teacher, a coach, a teacher in our public schools, a parole officer, or a concerned parent, we are much alike. I do not write to you as an academic or from some highly advanced position looking down on the underling novices. Instead I write while among you! I, too, share a love for teens and a belief that the work we do is some of the most important stuff that is being done on the planet.

As I write this, I am completing 10 years of youth ministry at the same local Nazarene church in Oklahoma City. Ten years of youth ministry in one place makes me somewhat of an oddity and a rarity—something in the Halley's Comet category. One of the benefits of being here this long is that I have been able to see beyond what is still an intrinsic pressure to "grow" into my next phase of ministry, that unwritten pressure youth pastors often get to move out of youth ministry and move into "real" ministry—pastoring a church. I've been able to keep my sights focused on all that we who are today's youth workers are trying to do in the name of Christ on behalf of the teens entrusted to our care.

Give me a good map, and I can get anywhere; without it, I am lost.

Having said that, I have a confession to make. (This is starting to feel like a support group!) I am chronically and hopelessly directionally challenged. My inability to drive a straight line between two points has become legendary. Let me show you how bad I am. Whenever I announce that I am off to anywhere in the city, my evil and heartless coworkers pepper me with the same questions every time: "Who's going with you?" "Do you have your emergency gear with you?" "Do you have any idea how to get where you're going?" Sadly, these are all pertinent and deserved questions. Recently I made an appointment to eat each week with a few of our high school men at a restaurant that is no more than 10 minutes away. We have now met four times, and I have yet to make it there on the first try. And yes, I completely fit the stereotype of the bull-headed, stubborn man who would rather pass a kidney stone than stop and admit my "lostness" to another human being. I simply have no sense of direction, none whatso-ever. Give me a good map, and I can get anywhere; without it, I am lost.

But I have another confession to make. My lack of directional ability is not limited to geography. About 6 years ago I awoke to the fact that, while I had some youth ministry talent and skills, I had no overarching direction. Sure, like every good youth leader, I had a set of goals that I wanted to accomplish. But I remember looking at the list I had prepared for my superiors and think-ing, "So what? What am I really trying to do in this ministry to teens?"

I don't claim to know what your goals are. But it might be beneficial if we look at some of the nearsighted goals I have had throughout my years of ministry. This will set the stage to help us understand what we should (and shouldn't) be doing in youth ministry.

When I started in youth ministry, my goal was to have a certain number of people in our youth group. I thought, "If I can only have X number of teens on Wednesday night or in Sunday School, then I will be successful. If X number of people show up for our next retreat, then I will know that God is pleased with my efforts, and I am being effective." I don't have to tell you that this was a misguided goal. Is there anything wrong with having a *huge* crowd in your ministry to teens? Maybe; maybe not. What was wrong with my goal was that I was measuring my (and God's) effectiveness simply by numbers.

After a couple of years, I got very deep and spiritual and I "divined" what I believed to be the perfect goal. I said, "This year I want to get this many people saved. I want to help this many people make a deeper com-mitment, and I want to see this many people called into ministry some-how." Now those sound like pretty good goals, don't they? Salvation and deeper commitments and people called into ministry—who would dare to argue with that? To quote one of the most quotable lines in recent adver-tising history, "It just doesn't get any better than this." Right?

But I vividly remember the day that I was finally able to be honest with myself, with God, and with anyone who might be watching, and I ad-mitted that I was getting nowhere. I wasn't reaching the numerical goals I had set for myself at the beginning of that year; I wasn't seeing lots of kids saved or called into ministry. So I started asking (and sometimes screaming), "God, what's going on? Are You not doing something, or am I not doing something? Whose fault is this?"

God was kind enough to gently show me that I had laid claim to some of His territory. Salvation is His territory; drawing people to deeper commitments—that's His territory; calling people into ministry really is His territory. I could and I should work to ensure that there is a proper environment for decision making. However, the commitments I would force people into making would remain artificial commitments. I have to admit that I was humbled. I was relieved to discover this, but I was also frustrated. *What in the world was I supposed to be doing?*

After much soul searching and listening to God, I finally have my answer.

So what are my goals now? I can best describe what my goals are now by way of an analogy. In the summer of 1999, my denomination (the Church of the Nazarene) held a massive event known as Nazarene Youth Congress (NYC). It's an event that occurs once every four years, and this time Toronto, Ontario, was our final NYC destination. On our way to NYC, we flew into Cleveland and then drove into Toronto, so that we could see some of the sights on the way. When driving from Cleveland to Toronto, you will pass Niagara Falls; there is no way around it. I had never been to the falls before; however, I had heard all about it. My parents spent their honeymoon in Niagara, and it seemed that many of the people from our church had been there.

When describing Niagara Falls, people almost always say the same things. First, you need to be on the Canadian side because it looks better from there. And second, make sure you stand close enough to feel the mist come off the falls and get at least a little bit wet.

Well, since I had never seen it before, I really didn't get what they were talking about. But, having this information in mind, I went to the Canadian side so I could stand close enough to get wet. Our whole youth group went. In our group there were some girls that didn't want to get wet at all. They wanted to stay out of harm's way. Now, depending on the wind, you might have to stand a long way back in order to keep from getting wet. If the wind is just right, and if you're really close, you can get completely drenched in no time at all. In fact, if the wind is blowing toward you off the falls, you can be standing a long way back and still get a little wet.

We also had in our group a couple of soccer players. I don't know what it is about soccer players. They're a different breed—they're nuts! Wouldn't you know it? These high-risk, high-adventure teens, after I convinced them that they couldn't actually get in the water, went over as close as they possibly, legally could and just stood there in that mist. Sure enough, they found a way to get every square inch absolutely drenched! Two of our teens, Tiffany and Brad, got so wet that we had to wait for them to change clothes. They were soaked through and through.

On the other extreme there was Brooke, one of my favorites. You all have a Brooke in your group. You know, the one who, no matter what time of the day you see her, six o'clock in the morning, twelve o'clock at night, in the middle of the night, she is spit-and-polished. "Don't touch me; my hair is just right. I've been up all night working on my hair." So, it came as no surprise that she wanted to stay far enough away that she could just kind of see it, but not really get touched by the mist.

That's my analogy.

Who would know best what the falls looked like? It would obviously be the ones who were the closest, the ones who were most willing to get close enough to get really wet. You see, because Tiffany and Brad were willing to get wet, they could tell us some intricate details about what they saw in the falls. These were details that Brooke would never know about because she wouldn't step close enough to the falls to really see it.

I see our experience at Niagara Falls as analogous to the way we experience God. I see the mist coming off the falls as the insight that is only available to those people who get close enough to God to be able to catch a real sense of who He is.

In Matt. 16:13 we read these words, "When Jesus came to the region of Caesarea Philippi, he asked his disciples, 'Who do people say the Son of Man is?'" When Jesus asked this, He was aware that there were many and varied opinions out there about who He was. People had heard the talk at the synagogue and in the marketplace. There was a lot of gossip about the miracles that Jesus was performing. Some believed that Jesus was nothing more than a nutcase doing some good things but also making a lot of people mad. And there were at least a few who had started to believe that Jesus was all He claimed to be.

The disciples replied, "Some say John the Baptist" (v. 14). Some of the people did believe that Jesus might be John the Baptist. They believed either that the reports of John's death were a hoax, that he wasn't ever really dead, or they believed that Jesus was some sort of magician, and He was John the Baptist come back from the dead. These people, safe to say, didn't get it! They weren't able to get close enough to Jesus to really see who He was.

Other people got closer, but they really didn't get it either. "Others say Elijah"—one of the greatest Hebrew prophets, the miracle-working prophet. "Still others, Jeremiah or one of the prophets" (v. 14). There were some people who got close enough to Jesus to see that He was mysteriously connected to God. They saw Him doing some pretty impressive and miraculous sorts of things, and they were just close enough, getting just wet enough to say, "Oh man, this guy is something special. Maybe this is Elijah or Jeremiah or one of the prophets." These were the people, the Jews knew, whom God had used to do His will. Maybe Jesus was another of these prophets. This guess was closer, but not close enough.

But Simon Peter had another answer. In my mind I can see him standing up, and I think there must have been a moment of pregnant silence as everyone looked at Peter, fearing what was about to come out of his mouth. He said, "You are the Christ, the Son of the living God" (v. 16). You must understand, this was probably not the popular opinion of the day. This probably was not the answer that most people would have given. But to this point there had been very few people who would allow themselves to get so close to Jesus that they would get all of the mist. Peter had gotten so close that I believe he could look at Jesus and say, "Knowing the Old Testament like I do" (we can assume that Peter had a working knowledge of the Old Testament because of other statements that are attributed to him), "as I look at You, Jesus, what I see is the next step in God's plan to come and gather us as a people. You are the Christ. You are the Messiah we have been waiting for."

"Jesus replied, 'Blessed are you Simon son of Jonah, for this was not revealed to you by man, but by my Father in heaven'" (v. 17). How so? Was it as simple as God reaching

My goal for youth ministry is to have my kids close enough to the falls, close enough to the presence of Christ, that someday the light will come on.

down and turning on a light? Possibly. But I think it was more likely revealed to Peter over the course of his lifetime as he recalled all the stories he'd heard from the Torah. As Peter reflected on these stories, and as he spent time with Jesus, God was able to reveal to Simon Peter, "You are looking at the Christ, the Son of the Living God."

Now, verse 18: "And I tell you that you are Peter and on this *rock . . .*" (emphasis added). I don't know how you have heard this preached or taught, but here's how I interpret this passage. What is the rock here? Well, obviously Peter's name means "rock," but I think that "rock" refers to Peter's understanding of who Jesus is. There's a difference. Look at that verse again: "I tell you that you are Peter, and on this *rock . . .*" In other words, it is Peter's understanding of who Jesus is—the expression of God, God himself—that is the rock the Church will be built upon. And the Church today is based on our understanding that Jesus was and is the Christ.

Now let me ask you, Could Peter have figured out who Jesus was if he had not gotten close to Christ? Maybe. I'm sure God could have revealed this information to him if He had so chosen. But I think the reason Peter was able to figure it out was that he had spent his entire life preparing for the Christ to come, and when He arrived, Peter took advantage of the moment to immerse himself in the presence of Christ.

My goal for youth ministry is to have my kids close enough to the falls, close enough to the presence of Christ, that someday the light will come on. I don't know when it's going to happen for my 12-year-olds or 15-year-olds or 18-year-olds. In fact, it may not happen when they are 21 or 31. But regardless of when it happens, I just want to make sure that they all stay close enough to the falls, and that I tell the Story well enough, that someday there will be an opportunity for that light to come on and for God to reveal himself to my kids. That's my goal. That's my direction! How will we do it? That is the focus of this book.

But let me warn you up front that many of the things we are going to be talking about in this book will sound more like a prolonged testimony than a skill-building book. Remember, it has not been too long since I wondered whether or not I was relevant, whether I was really getting through, whether I was making any kind of difference at all. The fact that my group was not growing explosively like I wanted it to, and whether or not that would be noticed and ultimately cost me my position, was beating me down. It wasn't that long ago when I finally said, "You know, God, I'm not sure if I can keep doing this. I want to be used like a tool in Your hands and see lives impacted and completely changed, and I know it can happen for teenagers since I have seen it happen before. But, God, I'm not sure if I am going about it the right way." And God began to talk to me about my direction.

During this time, Ps. 71 became a source of encouragement to me, particularly verses 17 and 18. As I was struggling trying to figure out what in the world I was supposed to be doing and what it meant for me to serve as a minister, this psalm really spoke to me. Hear the words of the psalmist: "Since my youth, O God, you have taught me, and to this day I declare your marvelous deeds. Even when I am old and gray, do not forsake me, O God," and here's the kicker, "till I declare your power to the next generation, your might to all who are to come."

As best as I can tell, the most important thing I can do as a minister to teens is to declare to them God's power and might. I'm just smart enough and have just enough faith to believe that God will take it from there.

I hope you will be able to see this book as being more about you, the youth worker, than about youth work. As you read this book, I want you to ask yourself the following questions: "God, am I making a difference? Am I doing what You want me to do in teen ministry? Am I working according to my own goals and plans and dreams, or do You have something to tell me? Is there something that You want me to be doing?" We have all been entrusted with this awesome responsibility to help people find God. As you read this book, it is my hope that you will understand how we can best do this.

Reflection Questions

1. What do you consider to be the primary purpose of youth ministry?

2. What are some of your goals for your youth ministry?

3. Does your current ministry allow your teens to "get wet" by getting them close to the Story? Or are your students only hearing about it second-hand because they are too far away?

4. Take a moment right now and ask God to open your heart and mind to what He might say to you as you read this book.

CHAPTER 1

AN

OVERVIEW

OF THE

WORLD OF

THE

MILLENNIAL

Youth workers of the world: I have a major announcement to make—*we are done ministering to generation X!* Now, before you get mad or write a nasty letter, let me explain. First, keep in mind that this book is aimed at those who are undertaking the challenge to minister to today's junior high and high school students. Second, understand that we are done ministering to generation Xers for a simple reason—they're gone. That's right, the last Xers have graduated from your group. Now a few of you may have an "academically challenged" Xer still in the room—he's the big one in the corner with more facial hair than anyone else. But he's the exception, not the rule! The Xers in your church are college age or older. They might already be Sunday School teachers. You may have Xers on your church board. Your pastor might be an Xer! Wherever they may be, they are not in the youth group anymore.

So now, youth workers, I want you to do something. Take all of your "How to minister to generation X" books, put 'em in a box, mark the box "Xer books," and shove it over in the corner next to your folded parachute pants, your Milli Vanilli albums, and that giant yellow comb that used to stick out of the back pocket of your pants.

And now, look around. We are all hip-deep in millennials! They're everywhere! You've seen them, but you may not have known what to call them. They've already been called everything under the sun: the Y generation, the 2K generation, the net generation, the echo-boom generation, and many other terms. Just who are we talking about when we say the "millennial generation"? They are only the largest generation of people since the boomers, a group numbering some 80+ million strong! We are talking about young people born starting in 1982, people who are today, at the writing of this book, either in elementary, junior high, or high school! (Strauss and Howe 1997).

Now I want you to be careful. Don't give in to the temptation to think that millennials are just miniature Xers. They're not! While they may share some of the characteristics and tendencies of their older brothers and sisters, they are already exhibiting some dramatic and exciting differences. Just to give you an idea of how young and different these kids really are, let me take a few moments to introduce you to the world of the millennial.

Beloit College in Wisconsin does an annual study of freshmen entering college in order to determine how these students differ from preceding classes. One of the ways they do that is to identify the major events, people, and places that the students of that particular class have little or no recollection of. The following is a list of their findings (this is going to make you feel pretty old):

- Millennials have no recollection of the Reagan presidency and very little of the Bush presidency.

- They were prepubescent when the Gulf War was waged. They look at the Gulf War and lump it into the same category as the Vietnam War—something that happened in the past.
- They were 11 when the Soviet Union broke apart, and they don't remember the cold war. They have only known one Germany.
- Bottle caps have always been screw-off, and they've always been plastic.
- Vinyl albums are antiques; the phrase "you sound like a broken record" means nothing to them.
- Many have never played Pac-Man; many others have never even heard of Pong.
- They have never played an 8-track tape. (And cassettes are obsolete!) The compact disc was introduced when the oldest millennials were one.
- Chicago and Alabama are places, not musical groups.
- Most have never seen a TV with only 13 channels. In fact, many have never known a TV without a remote control!
- They have never seen Larry Bird play basketball.
- The Karim Abdul-Jabbar they know is a football player.

Many studies have shown this generation to be one that values diversity, tolerance, collaboration, the family, and dozens of other positive, healthy ends. So, these are the wonder kids, right?

The best answer may be, "Let's wait and see."

Yes, as we look at the millennial generation there is reason to hope. But, right now, all we have is hope. This is a generation that hasn't grown up yet. And rather than hope, much of what is being written now about millennials is hype. In all honesty, I hope you will be careful not to believe all that is now being circulated about these millennials.

There seems to be developing two schools of thought regarding the millennials. One school is ready to crown the millennial generation as the next generation of heroes, a generation capable of achieving the greatness that the World War II generation achieved. The other school is not quite so impressed, believing that the only real differences between generation X and the millennials is that millennials have demonstrated better defense mechanisms. They believe that these millennial teens may not be any better than the Xers who preceded them. Chap Clark, professor of Youth and

Family Studies at Fuller Theological Seminary, may have succinctly summarized this position when he said, "Just because they [millennials] do not report discontent or rebellion doesn't mean they have none" (Clark 1999). Again, this generation is very young. They are not yet who they are going to be. Any responsible cultural or demographic study of the millennial generation would have to account for its youth, making room for what could be significant change.

Now that we have at least a beginning understanding of our ministry targets, let's get started. Remember, I want to challenge your direction, your operating system, as you minister to this millennial generation. I want to challenge not only how you're doing youth ministry but also why you are doing youth ministry. And with the information I will give you over the ensuing pages, hopefully I will be able to share with you how and why I am doing youth ministry.

There are specific reasons for the direction I propose we take when ministering to millennials. In order to build that case, we've got to start with a look at the world in which you and I minister to teens. Let me say this: this is not a sociology textbook. Like many of you, I have little or no patience for the endless stream of statistics that are thrown at us every time we work to understand a little more about youth culture. But it is often necessary to look at some of those statistics in order to get a well-rounded picture of what is happening. Over the next few pages we are going to take a look at society, at demographic information for the sole purpose of trying to understand what it is like to be a teen these days. We are going to do the best we can to put ourselves in their Doc Martens (a popular brand of shoes students wear).

Here is the first of three questions I want to ask you.

What if you were the teenager and you were the target of economic manipulation?

MARKETING IMAGE

I would submit to you that our teens have targets painted on them. The kings of the money world out there understand this as good business, to draw a target on moldable teens with "spendable" money. They have studied their craft well. They know what they're doing.

In 1994, Bob Pittman, then the chairman and CEO of MTV, was

asked this question: "How is it that you seem to capture the minds and the hearts of 14-year-olds? How do you market to a 14-year-old?" His answer was both profoundly true and chilling. He said, "At MTV, we don't market to 14-year-olds—we own them" (Campolo 1991).

He's right. They have figured it out. And they know that it has everything to do with marketing an image. Think about it this way—how do your teens spend their money? How and why do they make the decisions they make about the things that they will buy? My guess is that if you were to tell me how your teens spend their money, it would be drastically different from the way their parents spent their money and the way our parents spent money, and maybe even different from the way you spend money.

When my dad went out to buy a product, he bought it for its functionality; he wanted it to work properly, and he would take whatever image went with that working product. But so many of our teens are spending money in exactly the opposite way. More often than not, they are buying images, and they will take whatever functionality or quality comes along with the image of choice. Recent surveys seem to indicate that many millennials are beginning to spend for quality and functionality again. It is a discernable trend, but it is not yet the status quo. Most millennials are still buying for image (Tapscott 1998). It may not work at all, but if it looks right, if it carries the right image, it's likely to be bought by our teenagers. I don't know if Gap jeans are the best jeans in the world, but their commercials are pretty good, and they know who they're after. And as you read, no doubt you can think of a dozen commercials that shamelessly cater to the millennial hunger for image. When we're paying attention, we can see everywhere the question all of corporate business is asking—"How can we get our share of the teenage spending pie?"

The almighty dollar is the ultimate baby-sitter.

And really, there is good reason for this kind of target practice. In his book *Growing Up Digital,* author Don Tapscott references the findings of the Alliance for Converging Technologies. They estimate that American teens spend $130 billion (that's with a *b*) and influenced the spending of an additional $500 billion. So, in one way or another, teenagers in the United States in 1998 were responsible for the spending of $630 billion. Or to look at it in another way, teens influenced how 20 cents of every dollar were spent. Of course they will market to our teens! I would!

And stores are marketing to our teens. One writer described well how a Philadelphia-area mall became a purchasing temptation for teens: "Come see all the beautiful and exciting merchandise we have for you. Touch it, feel it, smell it, pick it up, try it on, need it, want it, pay for it with cash or without cash, now or later. It will make you happy, intelligent, accepted, pretty, loved, younger, older" (from William Ecenbarger, "A Nation of Thieves," *Philadelphia Inquirer Magazine,* November 29, 1987, 22, in Rainer 97, 90). The message is clear, "Whatever you want, just come get it at our mall."

Did you know that the average teenage girl in America spends $3,000 a year just on entertainment? I'm not talking about food and clothes, just entertainment. That's a lot of money (Katie Couric, *Today Show,* August 28, 1998).

AMOUNT OF DISCRETIONARY INCOME

Apparently they have money to spend. But have you ever stopped to ask yourself, "Where are they getting all of this money?" Look at the following table.

Teen's Money Source

Ages 12-17	Ages 12-14	Ages 15-17
Get it from parents	88%	79%
Occasionally earn from odd jobs	74%	70%
Get regular allowance	54%	29%
Have full- or part-time job	13%	33%

(ICR Teen Excel survey. Printed in *USA Today,* August 17, 1998. Copyright 1998, *USA Today.* Reprinted with permission.)

According to this article, 88 percent (roughly 9 out of 10) of 12- to 14-year-olds are getting money from their parents. But among high school students you would expect that percentage to drop dramatically, right? Wrong. Nearly 8 out of 10 high school students are also getting money from their parents. I was surprised at that last number—I thought there were more high school kids working across the nation than this, but apparently only a third of them are working full- or part-time jobs.

This says to me that the almighty dollar is also the ultimate baby-sitter. Look again—9 out of 10 junior highers and 8 out of 10 senior high-ers are getting their money from their parents. Mom and Dad, don't take this as parent bashing. I promise by the end of this book I think you will like me even better than you do now! The direction I'm recommending is an incredible thing for families. But the truth of the matter is that parents are busy. And when they can't spend the kind of time with their kids that they want to spend, somehow it feels like the next best thing to say, "Here's $20. Don't spend it all in one place."

And so we have teens running around with hundreds and thousands and millions of dollars to spend out there, and all of this before we begin to talk about the credit cards that are now available to your teens. You are aware of this, right? You can get a credit card as a teenager. And our teens are applying for and receiving their cards in record numbers. But it's not that they are somehow unaware that there is a price to be paid for running up credit debt. As a matter of fact, that thought seems to be nag-ging at them more than we might imagine.

UNCERTAIN ECONOMIC FUTURE

Our teens are aware that debt is a threat to economic future and health. Combine high debt, skyrocketing costs of higher education, and a job market that is becoming more highly specialized and limited all the time, and soon you will understand why many of our teens aren't too opti-mistic about their financial futures. They have begun to doubt that their parents' money will be there for them, and they have also become aware of a crisis with our social security system. We just thought they weren't paying attention, but they were, picking up a little bit from the news and a little bit from the newspaper and a little bit from overhearing us talking about it. Aware of at least a potential crisis, our teens no longer have the luxury of certainty when it comes to their economic futures. They don't seem to have the confidence that they are going to have as much as their parents have right now.

And have you noticed that these teens aren't good money savers? Unlike our parents who said, "We ought to save for saving's sake," these teens put money back if and only if there is something to be purchased: a car, college tuition, a trip, new Doc Martens.

Make no mistake. Money matters to our teens. Yes, I, too, have seen the retro clothes and old cars. But underneath all of that is a constant uneasiness, a mistrust of the economic system, and lingering doubts as to whether or not this race is one that can be finished, much less won.

Here is the next question I want to ask you.

What if you saw your family blow up or simply fade away?

"The United States has the highest divorce rate of any nation in the developed world" (Rainer 1997).

We have known this for a long time, but what does it really mean? How has it impacted and influenced our kids? In his book *Generating Hope,* Jimmy Long, a veteran college minister, quotes Steve Hayner: "This is a generation that women took pills not to have and a generation whose mothers have championed the right for abortion. Divorce rates have more than doubled in their lifetime. It's been an age where children have been devalued; where they have become latchkey kids who are expected to fend for themselves" (Long 1997).

The family used to be a place for belonging and nurture. But lately teens have languished at home while their parents were out pursuing the vanishing American dream. This is the generation that inherited the terms *latchkey kid, daycare kid,* and *home alone.*

A friend of mine recently made an appointment for his daughter to have her teeth cleaned at the dentist, and the following conversation took place between he and the receptionist.

Receptionist: "What is the patient's last name?"

"Curtiss."

"What is her father's last name?"

"Curtiss."

"What is her mother's last name?"

"Curtiss."

"Does she have any brothers and sisters?"

"Yes, a sister."

"What's her last name?"

"Curtiss."

This episode reinforces for me the idea that society simply expects us to come from broken homes.

Not all teens today have divorced parents, but they're twice as likely to experience divorce than boomers were.

We have one of those churches that has a nice sanctuary, so it's a place where people like to get married. And it's really kind of funny, and at the same time really sad, to see the bride and groom making their introductions at the rehearsals. "This is my dad, and this is my dad's wife, my stepmom; this is my mom, and this is my mom's husband, my stepdad."

Society just expects now that our teens will be coming from broken homes. What has that done to us? It has radically changed the way we define truth and the way we transmit values.

Youth workers, this is why you are seeing your teens redefine words like *family* and *home.* Now family is not necessarily the people who live under the same roof; rather the term *family* has come to refer to the people that teens care deeply about and vice versa. Home is no longer where you get your mail; home is where you find the comfort of belonging. It is now possible in some states for children to divorce parents. Teens who are willing to divorce their parents are teens who will adopt themselves out to the next group they believe will truly care about them. Our teenagers face money problems and family problems. What else could go wrong?

What if you lived in a world with no absolutes?

Have you ever heard teenagers make these kinds of statements:

"You believe what you want to believe; I will believe what I want to believe."

"You have your truth; I have my truth."

"That's fine for you, but not for me."

"If it works for you, great—but don't force it on me."

And last but not least, the champion word of the millennial generation—say it with me—"Whatever!"

I really think that economic manipulation is a serious issue, and obviously I think that the erosion of the family is a serious issue, and it impacts our teens. But I

> **Millennial teens are desperate to find trustworthy and reliable truth.**

really think that this third question may be the biggest one. In the mind of most millennial teens, there are no absolutes. And our teens are bouncing around, from different people to different influences to different ideologies, in a desperate search for real truth.

Recently I did a lesson series on the Ten Commandments. I had chosen that particular series on purpose because I thought, "Surely we will be able to dig down and find some kind of a foundational truth now. What danger could there be in teaching my teens about the Ten Commandments; it's not like it's controversial or anything, right?" On these tablets are some of history's nonnegotiables—don't kill, don't murder, don't commit adultery. So off I went, working my way through these foundational truths with my students, and on one particular Wednesday night I landed on the "don't kill" commandment. I was completely in my rhythm, a speaking zone of sorts, when suddenly a young man in the back raised his hand. My rhythm now completely destroyed, I breathed deeply and said, "Tracy, do you need something?"

Tracy said, "Yeah—I got a question. I understand what you are saying, and I can see where we shouldn't kill people, but what if by killing 1 person (who is a killer), you save the lives of 10 people? Or what if you are from another country, another culture, and in that particular situation or culture killing is just an accepted thing? It's like, you know, you get up in the morning and eat, and you kill somebody and go back to bed? Couldn't there be people in some remote country who have never heard of the Ten Commandments?"

I watched as faces in the room pondered all that Tracy was saying. Some smirked and went on, but others were now seriously considering what had been said! To use one of my favorite southern-fried phrases, "My ox was in the ditch."

You have to know Tracy. He is not one of those kids from a Christian, two-parent, all-the-time-in-church family. In fact, to this point Tracy's family has never walked through the doors of our church, much less attended one of our services. Tracy was and continues to be an outreach project, but in many ways, Tracy represents a lot of the thinking among teens out there. While challenging beliefs has always been a normal part of adolescent development, this generation of teens seems to be taking this practice to a new extreme, often challenging Christianity's long-held and cherished beliefs.

Please don't misunderstand me! Millennial teens are desperate to find trustworthy and reliable truth. This is why it seems that so many have been born to argue. This is why so many are willing to look anywhere and everywhere for truth, even beyond our treasured Judeo-Christian heritage.

When asked, "How do you know whether something is true?" the millennial teen is prone to answer, "It's true if it works for me." And what is most sad is that this view is not just limited to non-Christian students. When 3,795 Christian students were asked to indicate which of the following activities they had participated in during the last three months, a surprising 36 percent indicated that they had cheated on an exam or other evaluation (McDowell and Hostetler 1994).

And here we stand in front of our teens, claiming that Christianity is an absolute, foundational truth. "You can't argue with it; you just deal with it." And all the while our teens, even the church kids who have Christian families, sit up in their seats with their arms folded saying to themselves, "Maybe. But maybe not. If that's what works for you, great, but I haven't made up my mind yet."

There is nothing sacred anymore, not even those things long held sacred by the church.

When people describe this age of no absolutes, they often refer to it as the "postmodern" age. In short, this simply means that we have moved from the modern, Enlightenment views that were based on science and reason to an era in which emotion and intuition play equally valid roles.

Now don't get spooked. We aren't going too far into the ins and outs of postmodernity, but I wanted you to have a frame of reference when you read the term again.

So there you have it—the world in which you and I minister to millennial teens. It is a world where dollars have replaced bullets and missiles as the most powerful and oppressive tool on the planet. It is a world in which the constant attack on the makeup of the family has resulted in confused, damaged, and dying homes and lives. And it is a world in which, according to the millennial and postmodern mind-set, there resides no foundational, reliable, absolute truth—not even those things we have always held so close to our hearts.

Reflection Questions

1. What are some of the ways you have seen advertisers target teenagers? How do your teens respond to advertisements aimed at them?

2. How many of your teenagers come from divorced homes? What effect has this had on them?

3. Would you say your teens have solid values, or do your teens' values change with the situation? How many times have you asked them a question about values during a youth meeting and their answer was, "It depends"?

4. How are millennial teens different from when you were a teenager?

5. How are millennial teens similar to when you were a teenager?

CHAPTER 2

SNAPSHOTS OF

POSTMODERNITY:

THE

MILLENNIAL

MIND-SET

Now, in order to help us better understand this "postmodern" generation and the world in which our teens are growing up today, we've identified three major snapshots to give us a clearer picture of today's mind-set. See if any of these look familiar to you:

SNAPSHOT NO. 1: Moral Relativism

Have you ever heard of the term *virtual reality?* It refers to an artificial environment that you experience in your mind through the aid of a computer and special goggles. All the images you view seem real to your senses, and you can even manipulate them to some degree. But the truth is, the images aren't real. Virtual reality may be a pretty good way to describe how our teens feel about morality judgments. And it may well be the way an increasing number in our society determine morals and virtues and issues of character. They basically say, "If my senses tell me it's true, then it must be true. If my senses tell me that it is not true, it must not be true." Look at the following quote from George Barna:

> By an overwhelming margin, teens reject the notion of absolute moral truth in favor of a relative view of right and wrong. Three-quarters of all teens say there is no such thing as absolute moral truth; 4 out of 5 teens argue that nobody can ever be absolutely positive that they possess the truth of a situation; 9 out of 10 young people assert that what is right for one person may be wrong for someone else in exactly the same situation. More than 4 out of 10 teens go as far as to claim that you can tell if something is morally or ethically right "if it works" (Barna 1995).

While the people Barna surveyed were for the most part generation Xers, their views accurately reflect the postmodern mind-set of our millennial teenagers.

A roving reporter walked the streets in a northeastern city looking for answers to the following question, "How do you know right from wrong?" The answers are eye-opening.

- "Usually if you are doing something wrong a bell goes off in your head, and you just kind of know it."
- "I think kind of what feels right to us more than anything else."
- "I've always tried to stay away from absolute truths."
- "I can really think to a large degree back to the Golden Rule, that seems to be a touchstone for an awful lot of people, and if you carry it out, it seems to be a fair way to conduct oneself."
- "I tend to use logic as best I can. I do have moral absolutes, and they are based on my religious upbringing, which is Roman Catholic, but I do have a tendency to throw my own personal twist in a few of those."
- "I believe it is all in your heart what you believe is right or wrong. It can't be what the police say or what a judge says."
- "I think it depends on the way in which one lives. What may be right for me may not be right for other people. I mean, that's fine, and I don't have a problem with that. I think one has to define his or her own morals."

- "I don't think there is any such thing as an absolute, and I think that society basically tries to give you their beliefs of what's right and wrong, but really you just have to bring it down to what you believe to be morally correct for yourself."
- "I think a person should be able to do what they want and be able to justify it because they want to do it. I think people should not be very judgmental. I don't really think there is a right and wrong to anything."
- "I think there are some sort of morals, but in your mind you are the one who chooses what is right or wrong."
- "I have to judge what is right or wrong for me. No minister, no preacher, nobody can tell me that" (Boerner 1997).

Did you catch that? A bell goes off in my head? I throw in my own personal twist? Did it scare you when you read the response, "I believe it is all in your heart what you believe is right or wrong. *It can't be what the police say or what a judge says"?* (emphasis added).

Isn't it a short and slippery step from there to anarchy? If the police and the judge cannot tell you the difference between right and wrong, if you can always take that kind of decision into your own hands, then it is no wonder that a person can feel justified when he or she believes a situation calls for violence, right?

And how did you feel about the last response, "*I have to judge what is right or wrong for me. No minister, no preacher, nobody can tell me that"?* No pastor, no youth pastor, no volunteer youth worker, no Sunday School teacher is going to tell me right from wrong.

So, in other words, you the faithful Sunday School teacher can work all week and for hours at a time on next week's Sunday School lesson (you are working for hours on your lesson, right?); you can design the opening activity, the small-group questions, the wrap-up activity and gather video clips to add entertainment and credibility to your lesson; you can then stand up and present this irrefutable truth from God, and *still* your students are likely to look at you and mumble under their breath, "No

Your teens who are reflecting a postmodern mind-set tend to believe that the source of moral value judgments lies inside of them.

minister, no preacher, no teacher is going to tell me what's right and what's wrong." Or maybe, "That may be true for you, but my life and experience teach me something different." How can this be? It's because your teens who are reflecting a postmodern mind-set tend to believe that the source of those moral value judgments lies inside of them. Remember the quote from Barna we read earlier, "You can tell if something is morally or ethically right if it works"? The people that are in our care, in our pastoral care, are listening to us and not necessarily believing that we have bedrock truth for them. What a sobering, humbling thought!

SNAPSHOT NO. 2: Spiritual Hunger

But the news isn't all bad. The fact is, we have been dealing for a while now with a generation of teenagers that has exhibited a deep spiritual hunger. And while they may not believe in moral absolutes, they are looking for some form of truth. In fact, adolescents as a whole are one of the largest buyers of New Age spiritual literature. But the problem is that they aren't necessarily looking for truth as we understand it, and they aren't looking for it where we want them to look for it.

And when our millennial truth-seeker finds some nugget of spiritual truth that he or she likes or feels "works for me," it is put into his or her bag of spiritual truths. And then off to somewhere else, looking through a completely different source, finding a little bit to like over here, and that goes into the bag. This process is repeated over and over. And at the end of the day you have a completely individualistic, privatized spirituality that doesn't look like anybody else's spirituality. And this is completely OK with your typical millennial teen, since the source of all truth is internal.

I help out at a public alternative school. Not too long ago I was chewing the fat with some of my favorite kids when I ran into Josh. Josh is the son of a Baptist music minister. And make no mistake, Josh is a pretty smart kid; he is in an alternative school because he feels underchallenged in the mainstream school. And like so many others, Josh is pretty close to uncontrollable when he is underchallenged. Josh is the poster child for postmodern youth; he is smart, very well read, and very spiritually hungry. I'll never forget the conversation Josh and I had about faith. It went something like this:

"Josh, are you a Christian?"

"Yes, I am."

"Well, tell me about your faith a little bit."

"Well, I guess you could say that I'm kinda different."

"How do you mean?"

"I am kinda different because, you know, I really like Jesus and all, but, you know, I really like some of the things that Buddha has to say too. This Buddha stuff is working for me."

What he said to me next has stuck with me.

He said, "To be honest with you, I consider myself to be kind of a . . . Buddhist Baptist."

I haven't seen any of those churches out there yet—First Buddhist-Baptist of Oklahoma City.

Let's be honest, OK? Most of us are at least a little like that too.

In my church, the Church of the Nazarene, a church that I dearly love, we have a book we call the *Manual*. It contains many things, including our Articles of Faith, our church organizational structure, ceremonies of ritual, and other items. It also includes what we call our Special Rules. These rules might best be described as a "code of conduct"—things we Nazarenes should and shouldn't do. The truth of the matter is this: you will find very few Nazarenes who will look you in the eye and say, "I am thoroughly Nazarene, 100 percent. If it is in the *Manual,* I buy it." And my guess is that in your faith tradition, many feel the same way about your little black book or notebook or golden spiral notebook or whatever. More and more of us are like that.

But our teens have taken this concept and made it an art form. Your teens—even your raised-all-my-life-in-the-church teens are willing to look elsewhere for spiritual truth. They want the universe to make sense. They need the universe to make sense. And they are not convinced that what we are giving them is the sole source of truth.

In his book *The Ministry of Nurture*, Duffy Robbins makes this point with a great analogy. We have adapted it here in order to make our point.

When you were six or seven years old, you went off to camp for the very first time. And when you are six or seven years old and going off to church camp for the first time, your mom packs your suitcase for you. It's just the law of the land. Your mom packs your suitcase, and she puts the flashlight in there; she puts the Backwoods Off in there; she puts 14 or 15 pairs of underwear in there. And as you stood there and watched, you protested, "Mom, I'm only going to be gone for a week. I don't need 10 pairs of underwear! Give me 2 or 3 and let's go!" You can protest all you want, but Mom has the final say in what goes to camp in your suitcase. But as you get older, you have more and more say as to what will go into your camp suitcase. So the process goes, and by the time you're a senior in high school and going off to church camp, your mom says, "I am tired of fighting with you about it; pack your own suitcase" (Robbins 1996).

The same things happen throughout the spiritual upbringing of children. During children's early years, we tell them what to believe, and more often than not, they believe it. But as they get older, they develop these frightening attributes like independence and curiosity, and they start to window-shop at other places claiming to be sources of truth. Later they begin buying at those places, and soon they are buying there as often as they are buying at your place. And sooner than later, you have it—"cafeteria-style believership." It's like they're saying, "I like this; I like this; and I like this. I don't like this; I can only stand so much of this, and that makes me sick."

North America is not the bastion of Christianity that it once was or that many still claim it to be. Our teens don't have to look far to see a smorgasbord of spiritual beliefs. It is all around them. Did you know that there is a Hare Krishna temple in most major cities in the United States, as well as one in small cities like Moundsville, West Virginia? Did you know that there is an Islamic mosque in Cedar Rapids, Iowa? Did you know that Islam is the third fastest growing faith in America?

The man who used to be the head of the NAACP, Rev. Benjamin Chavis Jr., recently went to work for Louis Farrakhan, leader of the Nation of Islam. He has been quoted as saying, "Islam has given me a context in which to live out Christ."

Let me say it again. There is nothing sacred in this postmodern world we live in, not even our Bibles! The roving reporter we mentioned earlier asked another question, "What do you think about the Bible?" The answers to this question are proof positive that in our society, Scripture no longer holds the place of authority that it used to. Listen to these answers.

What do you think about the Bible?

- "What does it mean to me now? Not much really, I don't read it enough."

- "I think it is a marvelous document and well worth reading front to back."
- "It's a book. It's a storybook, and that's all it is."
- "It's an interesting book to read, definitely interesting. It's like any other book, it doesn't pull me in any direction at all."
- "I think the Bible speaks a lot of truth. The only thing I fear about the Bible is that people take things too literally and make it an extremist voice for themselves."
- "I think it is a wonderful book, and I enjoy reading it. But I don't have this feeling that it's the handed-down Word of God like some people do."
- "It's sort of a moral code, in a sense. I don't agree with everything it says, by any means."
- "I think it is a guidebook, and I think you need to read and interpret and study and decide for yourself what the message is."
- "The Bible, if nothing else, is a text that I think has meanings depending on the time in which one lives."
- "It's great fiction and makes for great study in a literary sense, but as far as what really happened, I would say it's way off the mark."
- "It's good and educational, and there are some moral values we should adhere to, but you cannot take it all literally."
- "I think it is interesting, and we have discussions about this all the time: whether it is real, can it be real, you know, and can people add to it. And I find it fascinating, and every time I get the chance to hear more about it or read more about it, I do, just from the standpoint of trying to ascertain how it came about and if it is real" (Boerner 1997).

Is it any wonder, when this is the attitude toward Scripture, that people are looking elsewhere for answers?

"You can't take it too seriously." "You can't take it too literally." "Great fiction." Again, George Barna seems to have found similar results in his studies. Consider the fol-

They're starving for personal encounters with the living Christ who makes a difference today, in the real world.

lowing quote: "From a spiritual point of view, the all-roads-lead-to-heaven mindset is widely ingrained. Half of all teenagers state unapologetically that it doesn't matter what faith you embrace since they all teach similar lessons. And millions of teens espouse the philosophy that it doesn't really matter what you believe, it's what you do that counts" (Barna 1995).

Our teens are looking for relevant, practical faith—the kind that "works" every day. So don't let yourself think that we are dealing with teens that have turned their backs on God. On the contrary, there is a measurable spiritual hunger throughout our society, and especially among our teens, that is a constant thumb in their backs to look, to search, to find out the truth. They're starving for personal encounters with the living Christ who makes a difference today, in the real world. They want an authentic Christ; they want an authentic Christianity; they want an authentic spirituality. But they aren't ready yet to believe that the Bible is the utterly reliable source of that kind of authority and authenticity.

Too often our teens have had good reason to resent the Church and its leadership. The lack of authenticity, or even the perception of a lack of authenticity, has made it difficult for the Church to attract and then keep millennials. What, then, can we do to make the Church more attractive? The answer to that question is in the third snapshot of the postmodern mind-set.

SNAPSHOT NO. 3: The Desire to Belong

If you're a youth worker, I'm sure you've seen our third snapshot of the postmodern mind-set. You work with it; you work around it. Sometimes it even works against you. What is it? That irresistible desire and need to belong.

EdgeTV recently released a video about belonging. One of the segments was an interview with two high school students. The first, an African-American, finds a place to belong in the Nation of Islam, while the second, a Caucasian, describes life after his family moves to a place where there is no church, no youth group to which to belong. EdgeTV does an incredible job weaving these two testimonies together to present the dilemma that each one of our teens will face at one point or another. Listen to what they say.

Caucasian young man: A lot of people think I belong.

African-American young man: I have joined the Nation of Islam. I am a processing member.

African-American young man: I have been invited to a lot of parties and been offered drugs and all that, but it is a fact that when you come into the Nation of Islam and you get discipline, they teach you how to discipline yourself.

African-American young man: I attended the march in 1995. I traveled with my brother.

Caucasian young man: It (the move) has caused me a lot of lonely journeys.

African-American young man: One thing I saw here was a lot of love.

Caucasian young man: No one to talk to, no one to relate to, no one to hang out with.

African-American young man: It wasn't your typical "Hi. How are you?" But immediately when I stepped inside, I was embraced.

Caucasian young man: I still know God is with me, but I still feel lonely 'cause I don't have human companionship.

African-American young man: We started moving past the Washington Monument, and there was like a little field there. And when we went over the hill, there we saw a sea of people, and I almost broke down to tears because that is one thing I have never seen before and one thing I will never forget. Walked down the street a little bit and saw some brothers from around the country and around the world, and they embraced me like I was their father or brother—like they knew me. And in a sense I guess you could say they did ("Belonging," from EdgeTV, Edition 19, IMS Productions, 1996).

Two young men, dealing with the same problem. Both battling this common disease known as loneliness. The Caucasian young man had recently moved. He had been taken from his peer group, his friends—the people who had been helping him scratch the natural itch to belong. The other young man, exhibiting the same desire to belong somewhere, scratched that itch by joining the Nation of Islam. Now don't miss the crucial point here. We have no reason to believe that this second young man went out, individual beliefs in hand, saying, "I've got to find a group that believes this and this and this." He didn't interview the Nation of Islam to see if all of the beliefs lined up and matched.

His first priority was to find a place to belong. The Nation of Islam said to this young man, "We want you here with us, and we can show you how, over a period of time, you can belong." He called himself a "processing member." And after he has been "processed," I guarantee you that this young man's individual beliefs will look just like the beliefs held by the Nation of Islam.

If you haven't heard me say it yet, hear it now, "Welcome to post-modernity!" Individual beliefs are flexible and negotiable. Here is how they will be determined. When that teen who is lonely searches around and finally finds a group to which he or she wants to belong, over a period of time, the teen will bend and flex personal, individual beliefs until he or she fits perfectly with the chosen group.

Because our teens feel isolated from and wounded by the adult world around them, they deal with their problems by belonging.

The Nation of Islam is doing something right. This young man found that deep sense of belonging that many of your teens are still dreaming about. Did you hear how he was talking about the people he saw at the Million Man March? He referred to them as fathers and brothers. He said, "They made me feel like they knew me." He found a place to belong in the Nation of Islam.

And now let me tell you something. If your groups, if your ministries to teens (whether you are in a parachurch ministry or working in a local church) want to have an impact on the individual beliefs of the students in your group, then make sure your group is an open, reaching, welcoming sort of group, the kind of place where meaningful and lasting friendships can be made.

The spiritual hunger we've been talking about is often satisfied just by buying into the beliefs of the group they feel they belong to. Now listen carefully. They may not initially believe what their friends are saying, but they'll adjust to it and eventually believe it because the desire to be accepted and loved is so strong. Because our teens feel isolated from and wounded by the adult world around them, they deal with their problems by belonging.

Have you noticed that teens today will defend the rights of any bunch of people to be a "group"? All indications are that this generation is the least prejudiced yet.

Regardless of what the group is about, teens are happy to celebrate their history and traditions and give them freedom to exist. Whether it's witches, Goths, jocks, Christian prayer groups in schools, or even racists, teens are saying, "That's who they are. They are a group. They can do what they want."

In many cases, teens have that attitude because they are looking for a group themselves! In an effort to find that group, teens today will gravitate to anyone who takes them seriously and validates the pain in their lives. In other words, *"I long for someone who understands me."* This is the message that they're sending. This is the thing they want most. Their friendships are survival techniques, and they'll crumble without them.

For years now we have been griping about the evils of peer pressure, as we have watched our students fall prey to drinking, illicit sexual activity, and other sins because "everyone else was doing it." But is it possible that peer pressure could work to our advantage?

Over a period of time, as relationships are begun and strengthened, your ministries could have great success in helping a student adapt individual beliefs to match those of the group. If we will do a better job at being the Church as God intended it to be, recapturing the closeness we see in Acts 2, then the teens in our care will begin to look more and more like Christ. And by the way, so will their friends.

Adoption precedes adaptation. Belonging precedes individual moral transformation. Count on it.

Reflection Questions

1. Think back to when you were a teen. Were the three snapshots discussed in this chapter relevant to you at that age?

2. In what ways have you seen your teens start the process of packing their "spiritual suitcases"?

3. How flexible have your teens been with their individual beliefs? Have you ever seen them flex their beliefs in order to fit in?

4. What evidence have you seen that your teenagers are spiritually hungry? How is your youth group helping meet that hunger?

5. How open is your group to outsiders? Are they friendly and welcoming to new teens? Or do they ignore or even shun visitors, making it difficult for new people to fit in?

CHAPTER 3

AN

EXERCISE

IN

BELONGING

Because I want to make sure that we have made this crucial point, I want us to do a little experiment. Let's pretend that I am a charming youth ministry seminar speaker from out of town, and let's say that you have called and asked me to come to your town to do my seminar. Because every good speaker wants to know his or her audience, I'll call and ask you a few questions about your town, so that I can get a feel for your area, your people, and for what it means to belong to "your kind of people."

Here's my first question. *Are there any festivals, celebrations, customs, or traditions that are unique to your area—so unique, in fact, that I may never have heard of them?* I've asked this question at each place where I've spoken, just to get a taste of the local flavor of a place. I'll never cease to be amazed.

In Alabama, people travel from miles around to go the National

Peanut Festival, where each year one lucky young lady is crowned Miss Peanut.

Ever heard of The Plymouth National Ice Sculpture Festival? I hadn't either until just recently.

How about The Hanover Tomato Festival? Nothing says party like the eating of tomatoes.

What about The Blessing of the Hunt in Wayne, Illinois?

I recently traveled to Conway, Arkansas, in early May to see some friends. It just so happened that I chose the weekend of Toadsuck Daze. It is a festival like you've never seen this side of Mardi Gras, and it's all about frogs and toads. Frog races, frog legs, frog show, frog clothes, and Toadsuck Daze T-shirts as far as the eye could see.

All of that fun, and to think that I would never have known about it if I hadn't been in town that one particular weekend. My life was enriched.

Think about this—if you were quickly able to answer that question for your own town or area, if you intuitively know about these festivals and these traditions in your area, you have successfully identified one way in which you can know that you belong to your town and to the group of people who live in that area.

Let's look at another question. *Are there any words or phrases that are unique to your area? You know, a language all your own, a secret code—something that someone outside your area would never know?*

A water fountain is a "bubbler" in Wisconsin!

Are you living in an area where people are "fixin'" to do something?

Here's one of my favorites. In Oklahoma City, Coke is the overarching term. I can go through the drive-thru at McDonald's and order an orange Coke. That doesn't mean they are going to blend Coca-Cola and orange—it is just an orange drink. What do they call it where you're from? Pop? Soda? Soft drinks?

Here's another one. *Is there any chapter in your town's history, your part of the state, that helps define you as a group of people? Are there names, places, or dates in your collective memory that are important to you, but that may have gone unnoticed or unappreciated everywhere else?*

For example, as one hailing from the great state of Oklahoma, I can tell you that in the 1800s, we had a land rush. People lined up for miles at the starting line just waiting for the gunshot that would signal the race to new land and a new way of life. But before that shot was fired, some cheated and jumped across the line. These people were known as Sooners.

Now there are a couple of stories that are more recent, and although they are tragic, we Oklahomans hold them very closely to our hearts. First, the bombing of the Murrah Federal Building on April 19, 1995. During the aftermath of that tragedy, there developed a great sense of belonging among the people of Oklahoma City because we had to close ranks to figure out how to cope, clean up, and live on after that bombing.

And then on May 3, 1999, killer tornadoes devastated the city. Again the people of Oklahoma City and the surrounding areas found a reason to lock arms and pull together. There was a sense of connectedness that allowed complete strangers to work tirelessly, side by side, as we sifted through the rubble of homes and lives.

We survived the bomb together, and we survived the tornadoes together. No, I don't yet know everyone around here by name, but I now know that we can work together, and I know that together we can survive anything life might dish out.

If you know the story line by heart, you belong.

What about you and your area? Is there a story, something that made news in your area that maybe we didn't know about? Maybe it was something that made national news, but only the people from your town knew the weight of all that happened. There are good chapters in these stories, and these are as important and as influential as the tragedies.

Can you see what is starting to take shape? We have talked about the traditions, the unique languages, and the particular, local histories. These are powerful ways in which you and your community belong together. You may not talk about it much, and you may not celebrate it; you may not even feel or even want to feel it. But I'm telling you, if you are from a particular part of the country, a particular town, or a particular part of the state, if you know these festivals and these traditions by heart and if you know the language and words by heart and if you know the story line by heart, you belong.

Now, let's take this understanding to a whole new level. It is my sincere hope and prayer that this book will be a help to youth workers in and beyond the Church of the Nazarene. I hope every one of our sister denominations can find something within these pages that will help win teens to the Kingdom. But in order for us to do that, I have a few questions that we all need to answer.

Do we belong together? And if we do, how can we know?

Well, let's ask the questions we asked above. *Do we have traditions, all of us who belong to the Kingdom that is and that is not yet, that we intuitively know about?* We don't really have to explain them to each other—we just know what happens. Isn't it possible that someone looking in on our unique traditions and customs from the outside may have no idea what the Church is doing? And by the way, those people still exist, people who don't know at all what we're about. Is it possible that there are some traditions we hold in common that an outsider may not recognize or understand?

How about Communion? Can you imagine what might happen if someone were to watch us eat what we call the Lord's Supper? I can hear it now, "That can't be all there is! Are there seconds?"

What about baptism? I know that baptism happens in many different ways in our differing traditions. We are dunkers in our tradition. I can only imagine what someone might think innocently walking in and seeing a baptism for the first time! Coming into the building to ask directions, he or she looks up, and there I am thrusting someone's head under the water! "Help, somebody call 911!"

What about a Good Friday service or a Maundy Thursday service or anointing with oil? Some of the things we do in the regular rhythm of being the Church make no sense at all to those people looking in from the outside.

Language is another way we can know we belong to a place and a people. When you use certain words and phrases that only your friends and family understand, you demonstrate the connections you have with those closest to you. I want to ask a question about language now. *Are there words and phrases that we inside the Church use on a regular basis that someone outside of our tradition may hear and not understand at all? Or is it possible that words we use inside the Church have a completely different meaning when used outside the Church?*

Here are a few. What about the phrases "I'm saved," "washed in the blood," "the blood of the Lamb," or "born again"? What about the word *grace?* Grace outside of the church might mean agility or athletic ability. Inside the church, it is the greatest gift given by our Father who gives great gifts! When we stop long enough to think about it, our language binds us together. We love some of those words and phrases; we've grown up and lived with these words and phrases. They have become both the system and the symbols of our belonging together.

But I have one more question. Do we have a shared history? Do those of us who are members of this global Kingdom known as the Church have any events in our shared past that bind us together? Sure we do! Don't get ahead of me. I want us to walk backward along our shared time line. Think fairly recently. What are some events in our recent history that are reasons in and of themselves that we belong together?

- The shootings at Columbine and the ways we have responded to them.
- The Supreme Court rulings about prayer in the school affected us all.
- Hitler and the response to World War II.
- For those of us living in America, the founding of our country at Plymouth Rock.
- The Reformation.
- The Crusades.
- Constantine's rise to power in Rome and his declaration that Christianity would be the national religion.

Keep pushing it back, back now into the pages of the Bible.

- The Early Church.
- Pentecost.
- The birth, life, ministry, death, resurrection, and ascension of Christ.

You're catching on now. Of all the great reasons we can name that we belong together, the biblical Story—the Bible—is the best reason we belong together. I would submit to you that if you subtract this from the equation, most of the rest of it falls to the side. I would submit to you that if our teens are going to feel like they truly belong to us, like I think I saw in that young man's eyes who found a home in the Nation of Islam, if we are going to be able to provide that source of belonging to our kids, it will be more because of this, our Story—the Bible—than it will be because of anything else.

You might now be saying to yourself, "You've got to be kidding. I paid hard-earned money for this goofy book just for you to tell me that the Bible is important?" It's not quite that simple. I'm not just saying that our history found in the Bible is important; I'm saying that our existence as a people is at stake, and our only hope of remaining and maintaining our essence as God's people, our distinctiveness, our peculiarity, our attractiveness to our young people who will outlive us, rests in our ability to retell the Story that makes us the people of God.

Do we know our own Story well enough to tell it?

I think that postmodern teens don't and won't believe that they can belong to the Church because we have not shown them how they fit in, and we have not demonstrated what the community of faith should be.

Has the Church abdicated its responsibility to be different from the rest of the world? Have we so sold our souls to the gods of popularity and "sensitivity" that we have become more tolerant than distinctive? Do the people inside our churches know what it is that makes us different, what makes us the "called-out people of God"?

And just as importantly (if not more so), can the people outside of our churches, those young people desperately searching for places to belong, those people begging for reliable, spiritual truth, can they look at us and see the kind of corporate identity and conviction we saw in the young man who was just a "processing member" of the Nation of Islam?

Do we know our own Story well enough to tell it?

Society has the answer for us. Sadly, they don't know who we are anymore. Listen again as our roving reporter asks what should be the single most answerable question in all of the Kingdom, "What is God like?" Their answers betray the mind-set we have been describing, and they betray the Church's failure to tell its Story in such a way as to describe the nature of God. Listen in.

What is God like?
- "I haven't the foggiest."
- "God is . . . Wow, what a question."

46

- "God is a higher power."
- "God is not a person per se. To me it is a spiritual being and no one knows. We all have these thoughts that, you know, whatever, if you are a Methodist, Presbyterian, Hindu, or whatever, but as far as God, he is an 'it,' not a he or she anymore. It is a spiritual being to me."
- "I am religious in my own way. I believe that there is a destiny for everybody, and you make it or break it yourself. You know what you follow is your own—but I don't believe there is a God."
- "I don't know what I believe in. I believe there is some higher power, I think, but I don't know. I mean, right now I'm at a point where I don't know what I believe, but I'm open to everything."
- "I have my own god. I don't really go to church. I used to when I was little. My parents stopped taking me, so I sort of developed my own god. I'm sure it is a combination of a lot of different gods."
- "I think of God more as an idea, and I think that it is an idea created by man actually."
- "I don't really believe in a Christian God. More and more I'm going toward the Buddhist religion right now in my life—enlightenment and nirvana."
- "God to me is this very mysterious character who keeps you in line."
- "I'm a philosophy major, and I'm heavy into 20th century with Nietzsche and Gadamer, and honestly I believe God is dead. And while I think that religion and whatever is important, I don't think there is a heaven that you go up to and there will be a god that is overlooking everything. I think that there is a being, but the basis of all being is a no thing—a nothing" (Boerner 1997).

The first time I heard those remarks, I felt like I had been kicked in the stomach.

Listen to these remarks. This poet seems to have nailed the picture of today's quest for answers to spiritual questions:

> We look for light, but all is darkness;
> for brightness, but we walk in deep shadows.
> Like the blind we grope along the wall,
> feeling our way like men without eyes.
> At midday we stumble as if it were twilight.

What a perfect description of all that is happening out there! What a perfect description of the millennial teens both inside and outside of your church walls! Can you name the poet? It must be someone who has been paying attention, right? It must be someone so inundated and haunted by the confusion around him that he can't help but describe it.

You might be surprised to find out that these words were taken out of the 9th and 10th verses of the 59th chapter of Isaiah. Amazing, isn't it, how much Isaiah seems to know our circumstances today? And lest we (the Church) should get too comfortable, believing that the confusion is limited to those outside of our churches, let us return to Isa. 59 to see if there is anything else for us to learn.

The 59th chapter of the Book of Isaiah begins with a stinging speech from God through the prophet, directed at the exiled people of Israel—God's chosen people. The people of Israel have been clamoring for rescue, relief from the hands of their captors. In the first eight verses of the chapter, rather than rescuing His people, God passes judgment on their ways. He accuses His people of rebelling against the rule of God for which they pray so desperately. He accuses His people of social injustice: legalistic oppression, unjust condemnation, and ultimately the deep social and moral apathy that makes oppression and condemnation a reality.

His angriest words were reserved for His people who had not been the "light to the nations" that He had hoped they would be. Simply put, His people no longer looked like His people. They no longer stood out among the nations. They looked like everyone else, and as a result, everyone else suffered.

Read Isa. 59 for yourself. Is our world in a similar state of confusion? Are we, the Church, in a similar state of confusion? Does social and moral apathy wear away at our distinctiveness and our peculiarity? Do we stand out anymore?

How do we answer the confusion?

Here's one way.

I believe in God the Father Almighty,
Maker of heaven and earth;

And in Jesus Christ, His only Son, our Lord:
who was conceived by the Holy Spirit,

born of the Virgin Mary,
suffered under Pontius Pilate,
was crucified, dead, and buried;

He descended into hades;
the third day He rose again from the dead;
He ascended into heaven,
and sitteth at the right hand of God the Father Almighty;
from thence He shall come to judge the living and the dead.

I believe in the Holy Spirit,
the holy Church universal,
the communion of saints,
the forgiveness of sins,
the resurrection of the body,
and the life everlasting.
Amen.

Do you recognize what you just read? It is a statement of belief. It is the Apostles' Creed—a rehearsed and refined listing of the most important beliefs that make us the Church. It is who we are at the core.

And it is a great answer to this age of complete confusion, this age that Isaiah would call the age of "spiritual blindness."

We can answer the world that has no absolutes by saying, "This is who we are; this is what we believe." Teens will listen to us if we're willing to truly see ourselves as the Body of Christ, a new culture, a separate community, a peculiar race, and a people called by God to *be* the people of God. You are working with a generation of teenagers who don't mind that you have an organization that has standards or a statement of belief. In fact, your teens like the idea of being a "processing member." They want to belong to a group that gives them an identity. And what is that identity?

We are the people of God.

Reflection Questions

1. What are some of the unique traditions that your youth group participates in? What makes them unique?

2. Do you know the meanings behind the traditions and rituals that the church calls us to participate in? Do your teens know why we receive Communion or participate in baptism? Have you ever discussed these topics with your youth group? If so, what was their reaction?

3. How can your group better assist students to become "processing members" of the church?

4. How can your ministry assist students to discover their identities in Christ?

**HAPTER 4**

WORSHIP AS

A RESPONSE

TO THE

MILLENNIAL,

POSTMODERN

MIND-SET

The truth of the matter is this—this era, with all of its warts and wrinkles, is the perfect time for the Church to be the Church! Not since Acts 2 has there been a better time for us to reintroduce ourselves to the planet as the people of God, a people of *worship!*

Worship! What a word! What a hot button! The word invokes images of the worship-style wars: slides or hymnals, drums or organs, ties or

T-shirts. Fixation on these details will derail the attempts for change. In order to make our mark in postmodern society, the Church must stop "underrespecting" worship and recapture its thorough, practical, and holistic meaning. In fact, the Church must fight its tendency to restrict the definition of worship to two hours on Sunday morning and one on Sunday night, or even more specifically, to the musical "praise" portions of those services.

Don't get me wrong. I love to sing. I love the "praise and worship" times in our services. Without a doubt, the musical, audible, corporate magnification of the Father is crucial to a healthy concept of worship. But to believe that singing completely captures the depth and breadth of worship is like believing that rap captures the entire essence of music.

We are in danger of missing the point. I believe that the Church's place in society is at risk. In case you missed it, churches are not the major, society-shaping forces they used to be, not even the really big churches! And in many cases, why should we be? Ministers have shown themselves to be capable of unbelievably sinister and tragic sins and in so doing have wasted places of influence and credibility, drawing skepticism and doubt instead. All over the nation, caught between the proverbial rocks and hard places, churches and their ministers are being relegated to the edges of society, with every step losing their grip on "mainstream" systems of thinking.

The problem is not that society sees all churches, ministers, and churchgoers as radicals or extremists to be avoided; society simply does not see the Church at all anymore. The only thing worse than being hated is being forgotten.

We are frighteningly close to being a nonissue, and again, our ability to influence and flavor the culture around us may be dependent on our ability to recapture a healthy, holistic, and *biblical* definition of the word *worship.*

This is an important chapter. The concept of worship that I am about to unpack for you is the backbone for everything else in this book.

How does the Bible itself describe or define worship? There are several Hebrew and Greek words that can be translated as *worship.* In the New Testament alone there are four significant words that can be translated as *worship.* Sometimes those of us who speak English get the raw end of the deal, and this is one of those times. Because we only have one word for *worship* while the Greek language used several, we miss out on the true meanings and nuances the original authors intended. Take, for example, one of our most treasured and often-quoted verses in all of Scripture, Rom. 12:1: "Therefore, I urge you, brothers, in view of God's mercy, to offer your bodies as living sacrifices, holy and pleasing to God—this is your spiritual act of *worship*" (emphasis added). Can this verse flesh out what is meant by the word *worship?*

Worship Is About the Story

Without question, this is one of the most influential verses in all of Scripture. But too often we don't look closely enough, and we cheat ourselves out of the enormous truth found in these words. For example, look at the first word, *therefore.* It's obvious that this word is referring back to something that was said or written earlier. But what is it referring to? What has been said to bring God's great mercy into view? What has been said that would merit our giving ourselves over as living sacrifices? Take a good look, and you will see what it is that has moved Paul to make such a statement.

This statement refers back to Rom. 9, 10, and 11, in which Paul walks through God's stormy relationship with His chosen people, Israel. In chapter 9, Paul begins by celebrating God's choosing of Israel to be *the* people of God. In Abraham, God's family is begun. It is continued through Sarah, Isaac, Rebekah, and all who would follow. Paul mentions Jacob, Esau, and then Moses. God's love and devotion to His people is the common thread that runs through this entire story, despite Israel's best efforts to rebel and frustrate the God of the promise, the God of the covenant.

Throughout the rest of chapter 9, and through all of chapters 10 and 11, Paul writes of a God who refuses to give up on His people—a God who time and again redraws the circle of Kingdom citizenship in such a way as to always include His wandering, chosen people. Nowhere else is God the "God of the second chance" like He is with

The stories of God's faithfulness and love are the inspiration and fuel powering true, worshipful responses.

the people of Israel. Finally, God redraws the boundaries of His kingdom in such a way as to include all who would call on the name of the Lord, both Jews and Gentiles. And *still*, God demonstrates the eternal "soft spot" He has for His original choice. "All day long I have held out my hands to a disobedient and obstinate people" (Rom. 10:21).

In chapter 11, Paul, a self-proclaimed Jew among Jews, still hopes and prays and strains and yearns for the redemption of His people. You can almost hear the hope in his voice! And yet, as Paul and God wait for Israel's hearts to soften, God in His mercy has made room for the rest of us to belong with those who have come to be known as "God's chosen people."

It is this mercy that moves Paul to these lengths. It is this unimaginable, unmerited mercy, seen in God's dealing with Israel and with all other people, that is worthy of an ultimate response from each of us. Paul, awash in this amazement, says finally in Rom. 12:1: "Therefore, I urge you . . ."

True worship arises because God has called and continues to call His people, the Church. As an echo, the Church's worship directed to God is a response to His gifts (Dawn 1995). Crucial to worship, then, is the Church's ability to remember and recognize God's gifts throughout history. The stories of God's faithfulness and love are the inspiration and fuel powering true, worshipful responses. But those stories are not just God's stories. They are the stories of the Church as well—they are *our* stories. The Bible records God's intention to seek and find and call out to us, the Church.

Not until we as members of the Church rediscover our Story, the Story of the dynamic relationship between God and His people, can we properly respond to God and His gifts; without our Story we cannot be living sacrifices; without our Story we cannot worship.

Can I be honest? Much of what is now called worship isn't really worship. At least not the way Paul is trying to describe it in Rom. 12. Much of what we call worship is more self-centered than it is God-centered. Listen to some "praise" choruses and you'll hear "Thank You, God, for what You've done for me. Thank You God for rescuing me. Thank You God for helping and healing me." Please don't misunderstand—those are songs that need to be sung. We need to sing our gratitude! But those songs must not overbalance the songs that understand God to be the God of the Bible—the God of Abraham, Isaac, and Jacob—even if my life never shows the evidence that God came to my rescue. Worship cannot be self-centered. God is not the ultimate vending machine. While God the eternal Father does seek to comfort His children, He is still God and still worthy of worship even if our "needs" aren't met.

What seems to be moving Paul to tears in Rom. 12 is not so much what God has done for Paul, but what God has done for humankind as can be discovered in God's salvation history as recorded in the pages of the Bible. Each of us has some idea of God's graciousness to us, but our perspective is hopelessly and helplessly limited.

Remember this is our Story, our shared experience, our shared history. It is what connects us to God and us to each other. It's foundational to who we are as a people. And if today's teens are ever going to feel like they belong to God and with us, they are going to have to own this Story for themselves. We want them to look at their Bibles and say with us, "This is our shared history."

It is in the Story that God can be seen for who He is and for all that He has done for all of us. That being the case, I'm not sure you can worship the way Paul describes it if you don't know your Bible—if you don't know our Story.

Youth workers, you have to teach our Story; you have to tell and retell our Story, or else your students will not truly know Him. If you don't tell the Story, they won't know how to be people of worship; they won't know how to respond! Worship is about the Story. It's about understanding and responding to all that God has done throughout the chapters of our history.

Worship Is Not a Religious Exercise— It Is a Relationship

Next, note Paul's emphasis on the nature of the sacrifices we are to make. They are now to be "living" sacrifices as opposed to the "dead" sacrifices of the Old Testament. The lives of believers are the only sacrifices desired by God, the only sacrifices worthy of God. For it is not in the dying, but in the living in relationship with Him, that we become acceptable sacrifices, holy and pleasing to God.

What does it mean to be a "living sacrifice"? Primarily, it means that we are continually giving our lives to God in order for Him to use us as He pleases. When we do this, our lives are no longer our own to control. We no longer decide what our future will be. Instead, we rely totally on God to lead us and guide us. We trust implicitly in His wisdom and follow His will as He reveals it to us.

> God has sought each of us out, interacting with us, building a heritage, a Story that continues to this day.

Closely associated with giving our lives to God is the idea that, as a sacrifice, we give God the totality of our lives. When a sacrifice is made, it is an all-or-nothing transaction. I'm reminded of the old story about the chicken and the pig. The farmer decided he wanted to have eggs and ham for breakfast. While the chicken was all up for it, the pig was a little more reluctant. When the chicken questioned him as to the reason for his hesitancy, the pig replied, "There is a little bit of difference in our sacrifices. What you are asked to give is something small. I'm being asked to give my all!"

Too many Christians want to be a living sacrifice, but only on their terms. They are willing to give a little, as long as it doesn't require too much. But the sacrifice God calls us to give is our all.

How can we give our all, not knowing what the future holds? The answer lies in the relationship. In what has been since the beginning of time a dynamic and living "relationship," God has sought each of us out, interacting with us, building a heritage, a Story that continues to this day. It is a Story that continues to be written through our lives as we live in relationship with this God of relationship.

Worship Is a Lifestyle

Paul says, "This is your spiritual act of worship" (Rom. 12:1). It is crucial at this point to recognize that the act of giving ourselves over completely as living sacrifices is equated with the Greek word *latreia,* translated as *worship* (Harrison 1976).

In the original Greek, *latreia* carried the connotation of service or religious homage. So with this definition in mind, Paul writes that believers truly worship when their lives are lived entirely *in grateful response* to God's nature, to His purpose, and to His good gifts that He gives to His people.

Eugene Peterson captures the essence of this lifestyle of "true worship" in his paraphrase of this same verse:

> So here's what I want you to do, God helping you: Take your everyday, ordinary life—your sleeping, eating, going-to-work, and walking-around life—and place it before God as an offering. Embracing what God does for you is the best thing you can do for him *(Rom. 12:1, TM)*.

The implications are clear: the "repossession" of our Story enables believers to recapture a way of life that has been dormant since the earliest days of the Church. The proper response to God will necessarily result in a particular, sacrificial way of life. True worship—the recovery and repossession of the Story, our Story—is a distinctive and peculiar way of life. Listen to the words of Craig Dykstra as quoted in *A Peculiar People*:

> In worship, we see and sense who it is we are to be and how it is we are to move in order to become. Worship is an enactment of the core dynamics of the Christian life. This is why worship is its central and focusing activity. It is paradigmatic for all the rest of the Christian life ... To grow morally means, for a Christian, to have one's whole life increasingly be conformed to the pattern of worship. To grow morally means to turn one's life into worship *(Clapp 1996)*.

Has there ever been a better or more strategic time to reintroduce to the world our peculiarity as the Church? In this age of tolerance and diversity, minority groups are singing their stories to the top of their lungs, reintroducing their unique beliefs and perspectives, demanding to be heard, accepted, respected. It is time for the Church to reembrace its minority status! With our Story, our characteristic language of love, forgiveness, and acceptance, and our peculiarity as a people firmly in hand, we can recapture our God-given identity, while enjoying the blessing and protection of postmodernity, the era of tolerance and diversity.

I think the Church was at its strongest and its most attractive when the people inside understood themselves as a functioning minority, and when the people looking on from the outside saw a peculiar and distinctive people. Look at this snapshot of our ancestors—the earliest Church:

> Everyone around was in awe—all those wonders and signs done through the apostles! And all the believers lived in a wonderful har-

mony, holding everything in common. They sold whatever they owned and pooled their resources so that each person's need was met. They followed a daily discipline of worship in the Temple followed by meals at home, every meal a celebration, exuberant and joyful, as they praised God. People in general liked what they saw. Every day their number grew as God added those who were saved *(Acts 2:42-47, TM)*.

> Our spiritual hunger is not filled by a religion, but by relationships with God and each other in the Church.

Does this sound like the kind of church you would like to attend? Do you think this kind of church would be attractive to your teens? These people understood themselves as a peculiar, distinctive people.

The climate is right, the time is right for a rebirth of an Acts 2 Church. We can be that kind of Church, we can again be the people of God, but it will not be until we completely repossess our Story! If we properly define worship the way the Bible wants us to, the way Paul is begging us to, then we will have the answers to the three postmodern dilemmas we identified in the previous chapter: moral relativism, spiritual hunger, and the desire to belong. Living life in worship, day in and day out with consistency, we experience the absolute truth of a loving God. Our spiritual hunger is not filled by a religion, but by relationships with God and each other in the Church. And since we are all looking for a place to belong, God has invited us to belong to His family. That's worth celebrating.

Reflection Questions

1. How has your definition of worship changed since reading this chapter?

2. What role does worship currently play in your youth ministry? If you were to tell your teens, "Tonight we are going to worship," what would their expectations be?

3. Do you believe that leading your teens in a Bible study, where you are retelling some part of the Story, is actually worship? Does this change your thinking about how you should go about preparing for each week?

4. If you were to adopt the view of worship as presented in this chapter, how would your youth ministry need to change?

CHAPTER 5

TRUE NORTH:

THE

DIRECTION

OF WORSHIP-

CENTERED

YOUTH

MINISTRY

We have already discussed my handicap—I am directionally challenged. I'm wondering if there are any others out there? Let's find out. Wherever you are today, whether you're in your home or your church or your office, can you point north? Do you know which direction is north? As silly as it may sound, and as silly as you might feel doing this, I'm going to ask you to do a little experiment. In a moment, after I've finished giving you a few directions, I want you to put down this book and walk to a place in your home or office where you can find enough space for you to spin! When you get there I want you to close your eyes, spin for 30 seconds, and stop. You can spin as fast as you like, or as slowly as you like, as long as you keep your eyes tightly shut. When you stop, without opening your eyes, point in the direction you now feel to be north. Go ahead. Try it. I'll be here when you get back.

> It is through authentic worship, the Story, the relationships, and the lifestyle that we find our True North— the God of the Story, the God of our Story.

Well, how did you do? Did you nail it? Not me, given my sense of direction, and especially not after spinning for 30 seconds.

I know you're asking, "OK, Jon. What's the point? Why did you get me dizzy?" The point is this. Though you and I may have been confused and disoriented, though we may have missed when trying to identify north, the reality of north remained. Its direction had not changed regardless of where we were pointing.

I thoroughly enjoy doing this little experiment with groups of people. After spinning for 30 seconds, there is some moaning and groaning, at least a little listing, and no end to the varying interpretations of north. But the point is crucial: regardless of how any of us might feel at any given time, regardless of what our opinion might be, the reality of the direction of north never changes. In this age of seemingly no absolutes, we have found one—"North is _____ way." (You fill in the blank by pointing.) Your church board could get together and vote unanimously to change the direction of north, but it won't work. It'll still be _____ way. Congress could vote, but it wouldn't change the reality of where north actually is. North is unchanging. North is reliable. The reality of north is crucial to navigation.

Youth workers, maybe you are like me. I have always worked pretty hard. I have been trying to run the race, but I haven't always known how to navigate, how to find my direction. I haven't always known which way was the True North.

The reality of a True North gives context and meaning to where we are, where we are going, and how to get there. True North gives us a point of reference, a place to aim.

In this book I have been describing a True North that can orient our ministries and help us navigate our teens toward a repossession of our identity as the people of God. It is through authentic worship, the Story, the relationships, and the lifestyle, that we find our True North—the God of the Story, the God of our Story.

Worship can be the compass by which we navigate youth ministry as we try to lead our teens back to our True North. Worship can and should guide our steps and flavor our ministries. Anything and everything we want to do for teens can be done under the influence and leadership of authentic worship.

That being the case, I want to introduce what may be some new terms to you. These are new ways of looking at old youth ministry challenges.

These terms are:

1. Worship-Centered Teaching—How will I retell the Story to the teens entrusted to my care?
2. Worship-Centered Community—How will the Story affect the way we connect to one another?
3. Worship-Centered Reflection—How will we live out this Story for all the world to see?

Is there another way to do youth ministry? Can the Story found in the pages of the Bible really influence the way you are doing youth ministry? Yes, it can! Let's find out how.

Reflection Questions

1. Why is it important to have a point of reference, a place to aim, for our youth ministries?

2. What is the True North that currently guides your youth ministry?

CHAPTER 6

WORSHIP-CENTERED TEACHING

Do you travel by plane very often? The better question is this: have you flown often enough now to be able to completely ignore the flight attendant as he or she acts out the safety speech? (A list of helpful, potentially lifesaving tips for you and everyone else on the plane.) The last time I flew, I was struck by my own ability to completely tune out this information that, in a serious pinch, could save my life!

Here was this woman at the front of the plane doing her job, and doing it respectably well. She utilized visual aids in her presentation and had a very pleasant facial expression, all keys to effective public speaking. There she was, giving us lifesaving instructions. And there I was tuning into my sports section while other passengers talked among themselves, slept, wrestled with children, or started on crossword puzzles.

The truth is that we are doing everything but listening. As I've thought about this, I've decided there must be two reasons why. First, we really don't think the plane is going down. If we had believed that to be even a remote possibility, we would have opted for a car, a boat, a train, a mule—any other form of transportation but that plane. And second, if by some horrible accident this plane were to go down in flames, we're pretty sure that putting our heads between our knees will do us absolutely no good. If I'm flying over mountain ranges, the fact that my seat is a flotation device isn't of much help to me.

When you're up front speaking to your teens, do you ever feel like a flight attendant? Do you ever come to your meeting, visual aids in hand, only to have your audience talk, nap, and look for crossword puzzles? Do you wonder why? It's the same reasons you have for ignoring the flight attendant. First, they're not convinced that utter disaster is just an accident away. Second, if that accident does take place as it has for more and more of our teens, they are nowhere near convinced that the stuff we're dispensing is lifesaving information.

Therefore, I propose that the biggest problem we have as those who minister to teens is that we don't teach the Bible the way it needs to be taught.

Worship-Centered Teaching . . . *retells* the *biblical Story*.

Look at the following example from the 8th chapter of the Book of Acts. God is talking to Philip and He says in so many words, "I want you to go to this place where someone is about to pass by, and I want you to talk to him." So Philip went where God wanted him to go, and sure enough, an Ethiopian eunuch passed by. Now before we go any further, let's wipe that smirk off your face. I have studied that word *eunuch,* and it turns out that there are a couple of meanings. For the purposes of this discussion, a eunuch is an official in the government, a worker in someone's Royal Cabinet.

So our character in this story is a member of the royal cabinet of Candace, the queen of the Ethiopians. He is the treasurer, the check writer, if you will. Philip walks up and sees this man reading the Book of Isaiah the Prophet. And the Spirit told Philip, "Go to that chariot and stay near it."

Notice that this Ethiopian eunuch is exhibiting some pretty teenage-like tendencies. He is curious, and he has some sense that there is something here in the Book of Isaiah that is worth reading, but he doesn't understand at all what he is reading. There is reason to believe that this man was a well-read, cosmopolitan, all-around pretty smart guy. It should be no surprise to us that such a man, being in the spiritual headquarters of the Jews, would want to familiarize himself with the Jewish faith.

I recognize also in this young man the same thing that Philip recognized as he approached and heard the man reading — a spiritual curiosity. He happened to be reading a classic. He "was reading this passage of Scripture [from the prophet Isaiah]: 'He was led like a sheep to the slaughter, and as a lamb before the shearer is silent, so he did not open his mouth. In his humiliation he was deprived of justice. Who can speak of his descendants? For his life was taken from the earth'" (Acts 8:32-33).

Philip ran up, heard the scripture being read, and asked the man if he knew what he was reading. The Ethiopian man responded, "How can I, . . . unless someone explains it to me?" (v. 31). He then goes on to say, "Tell me, please, who is the prophet talking about, himself or someone else?" (v. 34).

Now here is the crucial point, found in verse 35: "Then Philip began with that very passage of Scripture and told him the good news about Jesus."

Did you catch it? Look at it again. "Then Philip *began with that very passage of Scripture* and told him the good news about Jesus" (emphasis added). I want that to sink in. I want that to wrap around your throat. How can you make the case for Christ the way God wants the case to be made for Christ if you do not use the Old Testament? I don't pretend to know how long they traveled together or what he said, but I'm telling you he had to at some point retell the entire Story (which is also our Story) in order to make Christ's sacrifice make sense!

Apparently this was a long chariot ride. Philip seems to have had time to work all the way through the Story and into the rituals and cere-monies whereby persons are initiated into the Story. And Philip made the case so well that the Ethiopian man jumped at the first opportunity to be baptized. "As they traveled along the road, they came to some water and the eunuch said, 'Look, here is water. Why shouldn't I be baptized?' [Philip said, 'If you believe with all your heart, you may.' The eunuch an-swered, 'I believe that Jesus Christ is the Son of God' (margin)].

"And he gave orders to stop the chariot. Then both Philip and the eu-nuch went down into the water and Philip baptized him. When they came up out of the water, the Spirit of the Lord suddenly took Philip away, and the eunuch did not see him again, but went on his way rejoicing" (Acts 8:36-39).

Do you know when you teach and preach the Story as it is intended to be taught and preached, it changes hearts and minds and lives? You can have someone walk into your ministry confused, beat up, burnt out, bedraggled, and he or she can leave your ministry—if you have been faithful to transmit the Story of God—rejoicing, even if you disappear!

If it were your responsibility to tell the Story of God to someone who had never heard it before, what stories would you believe to be the most crucial?

The Bible has great transformational power. But you already knew that, right? Then why is it that you and I have had a tendency to rob the Story of its power?

Allow me to step on your toes a little bit. And as I do this, please know that my own toes are eternally scarred. Here's a question: How do you teach the Bible? You really have two options.

First, there is the topical method. This is where you try to discern what the needs of your teens are and then search the Bible for answers to those needs. You say, "Our kids are struggling with sexual purity, so we are going to teach on sexual purity today." And then the next week you might say, "I heard that some of our kids are struggling with their parents, so we are going to teach '5 Ways to a Better Relationship with Mom and Dad.'" Then you might say, "Our young people obviously are struggling with self-image, so over the next few weeks we will work through '12 Steps to a New You.'"

Please understand that I am not here to bash topical teaching. My primary concern with topical teaching is that most youth workers move from topic to topic, without any real sense of direction or purpose. Too often, youth workers simply return to their pet topics time after time because that is what they feel comfortable teaching. And as a result, the teens under their care do not receive the full Story of God, but only those bits and pieces that the youth worker feels are important. In the end, without a real plan to guide them, most youth workers cheat their students out of really discovering what God's Story is all about.

The other method is what I term the "Preventive Medicine" approach to teaching Scripture. I did a little bit of checking to see how the ancient Israelites taught their children. Without many of the wonders of technology that more and more of us have at our disposal to transmit biblical truth, how did the ancient Israelites teach faith to their children?

They told stories. They told them in a particular order so as to build their children from the inside out.

I haven't always done that in my youth ministry.

Mind if I pry a little? Do you know what you are going to be teaching on Sunday? Do you know what you are going to be teaching a week from now, a month from now? Do you have an overall strategy so that you know what you are teaching for this semester or even for the entire year? Do you have *any* kind of strategy? If you are anything like me, even as recently as four years ago I would have answered most of these questions with the ever-frustrating, "I don't know."

If you are like most Sunday School teachers, you may skip and jump around from topic to topic. Let me tell you. I don't let my Sunday School teachers write their own curriculum. Why? Is it because I don't trust them? Of course not! If I didn't trust them, I wouldn't have asked them to teach! But I supply their teaching texts because I want to be sure that we are taking every opportunity to retell the biblical Story for our teens.

Let's talk about the Story of the Bible. Look at the time line that has been provided for you (see Appendix A). Let that time line represent the story line in the Bible. Take a few moments to put Creation at the beginning and the Second Coming at the end. Now, I would like for you to answer the following question: If it were your responsibility to tell the Story of God to someone who had never heard it before, what stories would you believe to be the most crucial? We want to completely cover what it means to be the people of God. Which biblical stories are the non-negotiables? Go ahead, take a few minutes, and write these on the time line. Do your best to try to keep the stories in order.

Done? OK. Here are some of the stories that I considered to be the most important. Check to see how close your list matches mine.

- The Fall—Sin bursts onto the scene.
- Abraham—Our father of faith. The original keeper of the promise. The father of Israel. Abraham is so very important. I want my teens to sense that we together are the people of God, and that our people in so many ways begin with an old man who dared to trust God.

67

- Isaac.
- Jacob.
- Joseph.
- The Exodus—God rescues His people.
- Sinai—The Ten Commandments—God shows His people how they can continue to be the distinctive, peculiar people of God.
- Israel demands a king.
- Israel has good kings and bad kings.
- King David.
- Exile—Israel suffers the consequences of wandering away from God.
- Restoration.
- The birth, life, ministry, death, resurrection, and ascension of Jesus.
- Pentecost—The birth of the Church and the giving of the Holy Spirit.
- Paul's ministry in the Early Church.

This is the end of biblical time. But now your time line should show a gap between the end of biblical time and the Second Coming. Do you know what belongs in that space?

We do. That is where we live now, you and I, as we minister to our teens. Why is that so important? Let me tell you something. Your kids won't truly belong the way God wants them to belong, and the way that they want to belong, until they know that they belong on this time line right here with the likes of Abraham, Moses, and Jesus Christ, all members of the family of God. If we'll do this thing right, we can show them how they can be a part of God's Story—the Story that continues to be written through us by God.

Several of us were together struggling with this very issue. We could tell that we were on to something, but we couldn't figure out how to talk about it. We were in a fifth grade boys' Sunday School classroom in a church in Olathe, Kansas. And there we were, pulling our collective hair out when someone tapped me on the shoulder and said, "Look at the wall." On this particular wall was a time line. It was one of those little Sunday School curriculum, flannel-graph-looking, cartoonish time lines, but it had all the highlights: creation, Fall, Noah, Abraham, Isaac, Jacob, Joseph, Moses, David, the Exile, Jesus, Pentecost, and a picture of the Second Coming at the far end.

Taped in the space between Pentecost and the Second Coming, there it was — a Polaroid snapshot of the fifth grade boys in that class. It had been there all along, but until then, we had been too blind to see the simple and yet crucial truth hanging on the wall.

That brilliant teacher is on her way to giving those boys the gift of belonging in the biblical Story. And as we discover our places in the Story, we find our own identity and the kind of responsibility that comes along with being a part of that biblical Story — the kind of identity and belonging and responsibility that will preserve our tradition for years.

Are you with me? It matters that Moses follows Abraham. It matters that Christ is an expression of all that has gone before. It matters that Pentecost follows the ascension of Christ. It all matters. But I didn't always teach like it mattered. Because I had no overall sense of what the Story was about, I had a hard time giving my teens an overarching sense of all that God has been doing in and through history. And believe me, God is definitely up to something.

Worship-centered teaching means that you tell the Story of God in such a way that it demonstrates two things: first, that God is up to something; second, that we can help!

Worship-Centered Teaching . . . is more active than passive.

Dead Poets Society is one of my favorite movies. In the movie, Mr. Keating (played by Robin Williams), a popular English teacher at a private high school in the northeastern part of the country, jumps up on his desk and asks his class, "Why do I stand up here?"

"To feel taller?" one of his students replies.

Keating answers, "No! I stand on my desk to remind myself that we must constantly look at things in a different way. See, the world looks very different from up here. You don't believe me? Come see for yourselves. Come on. Just when you think you know something, you have to look at it in a different way. Even though it may seem silly or wrong, you must try."

This clip makes an incredible point. In order for our students to truly see what God has in store for them, for them to understand what it means to participate in His Story, we need to help them gain a new perspective. We must move them from being passive observers to being actively involved in the teaching and learning process.

Mr. Keating could have made his point without climbing up on his desk. These students were used to the lecture style of teaching. They were getting it everywhere else! And Mr. Keating could have stopped with jumping up on his own desk. Already he was out of the ordinary and above average. But it wasn't enough for Mr. Keating to tell them, and it wasn't enough for Mr. Keating to show them; he wanted his students to see for themselves. So what did he do? He invited the entire class, one at a time, to jump up on his desk and take a fresh look at the classroom. He wanted them to be participants in the learning process, not just spectators.

Worship-centered teaching is in its essence more active than passive. The traditional lecture style is a passive form of teaching and learning. And you know, from painful experience, that the lecture style is not always the best way to get your point across. And here's proof. Look at the two diagrams provided below. These are from a study done by Edgar Dale:

THE CONE OF EXPERIENCE

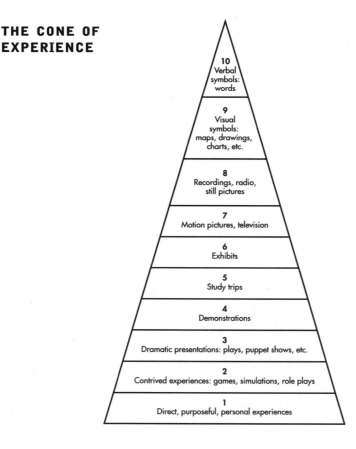

10
Verbal symbols: words

9
Visual symbols: maps, drawings, charts, etc.

8
Recordings, radio, still pictures

7
Motion pictures, television

6
Exhibits

5
Study trips

4
Demonstrations

3
Dramatic presentations: plays, puppet shows, etc.

2
Contrived experiences: games, simulations, role plays

1
Direct, purposeful, personal experiences

THE CONE OF EXPERIENTIAL LEARNING

5-10% Verbal or written

25% Media

40-60% Role play

80-90% Experience

Charts from *Audio Visual Methods in Teaching.* Third Edition by Edgar Dale, copyright © 1969 by Rinehart and Winston. Reproduced by permission of the publisher.

Edgar Dale's work is of monumental importance to us who teach. When we look at these diagrams we discover that when we try to teach by only expressing our point verbally or by writing it on a board or a piece of paper, we are making a minimal impact. In fact, for every 100 words that we speak or write, our teens are only catching 10 if we're lucky. Only 10 of our words are making any impact at all.

And so we try to get a little creative. We go out and buy cool bells and whistles like PowerPoint. We do this in order to up the ante, to try and capture our teens' attentions. But even then our teens are only picking up a whopping 25 out of every 100 words.

Now, we get serious. We get them up and out of their seats to do a little role-playing, and still they take home only 40 to 60 percent of the things we are trying to say.

Now look at that bottom line in the table. When we can actually figure out a way for our teens to experience the truth of the lesson in a hands-on way, then they take home 80 to 90 percent of the lesson we're trying to get across.

It is not enough to say, "As Christians, you should go and feed the poor." Instead, after you teach that lesson, go and serve in the soup line at the city's rescue mission. Go and help feed the poor! I know it sounds simple, but we act as if it is nearly impossible.

Sometimes the best thing you can do for your teens is to cancel your regularly scheduled activities so that you can give your teens an opportunity to experience the truth of a lesson. You'll be amazed at what you can teach and what your teens can learn.

Worship-Centered Teaching . . .
is more *we-oriented* than *I-oriented*.

The focus of worship-centered teaching is not on the individual but on the community. It is this kind of emphasis that will tie our students to the traditions of the Church and the depth of the Scripture.

As we've said before, in order to belong, a teen is willing to bend his or her individual beliefs to match those of the group. That being the case, this is the perfect time to say, "Here is a place to belong, and here is how we believe." This doesn't mean that we seek to take advantage of this desperate desire to belong and so create students who appropriate our beliefs but fail to live them out. What it does mean is that we can provide a place where students can feel welcomed and accepted. And when the students make the choice to enter our groups, we can then stand up and say, "This is who *we* are and this is how *we* believe." Worship-centered teaching does not apologize for having distinctive beliefs.

Here's what I mean. We need to get better at saying, "This is who we are without apology." We need to be better at saying, "These are the foundational things that we believe as a community of faith." It is not our job at this point to try and prove that other beliefs are wrong. Instead, we simply say, "This is who we are. And while we definitely want you to belong with us, we want you to know, before you make that decision, that this is who we are."

I know that this sounds a little harsh, but it demonstrates a commitment to our core convictions, an attitude that will be attractive to the typical millennial student who is searching for a legitimate place to call his or her spiritual home.

Another aspect of being more we-oriented than I-oriented is in how we assist our teens with their devotional lives. We all know that a regular devotional time is essential to the development of faith. And because we know this, I want to help us think about how we can best assist our students in doing their devotions.

It could be that some of you, in an effort to provide devotional material for your students, have created your own booklets and sheets that your students can use. I also have created similar things for my students. Not too long ago, I created what I thought were the coolest things I had ever seen, an artistic and technical marvel, and from my own limited hands. These were the perfect devotional sheets—the perfect tool to help develop saints. See if what I describe sounds familiar to you.

The presentation was stunning. I had placed our supercool "Fresh Fish" logo in the top right-hand corner of the page. Then in a complementary font, I had provided my students a place to write in the date and the scripture reference for the passage they had chosen to read on that particular day. Then I carved out creative space on that same page, room enough for my students to answer the following questions: "What does this scripture mean to me?" and "How can I apply this to my life?"

Sounds pretty good, doesn't it? I was so pleased with what I had created.

But I have to tell you that I was wrong. The pages asked the wrong questions. The design, while stunning, was wrong.

I missed it. I was asking my teens questions they had no business answering, putting them in places of authority and experience before they were ready to be there. Now don't misunderstand me. My heart was right. I wanted to get my kids into the Word, and I wanted them to pray, so I sought to help them by giving them resources for recording their scripture insights and prayers. I was trying to do the right thing, but I wasn't doing anything that even resembled worship-centered teaching.

The disciplines I recommended to my students were totally I-oriented. Basically what I was doing was giving the sheets to my teenagers and saying, "You tell me what you want to read. What's your favorite verse? John 3:16? OK, you can read it every day if you want. Now, what does it mean? No, really, I want you to tell me what it means. Don't worry about what others think. This is just between you and God."

Let's be painfully honest with one another. My teens and your teens are nowhere near equipped to be the final authority on the interpretation of Scripture, and we do them a great disservice when we look at them and ask, "What does that scripture mean to you?" as if Scripture is open to any and every teenage interpretation! You do realize that it is possible to misinterpret the Bible. And in fact, the young people entrusted to our care may be more prone to misinterpret Scripture because they simply don't have the wisdom to always interpret it correctly.

Youth worker, *it's your responsibility* to open the Scriptures for your teens and tell them what these passages are trying to get across. *It's your responsibility* to guide and shape and even correct your teens when they have misinterpreted Scripture.

In the sheets I had designed for the students, I had asked another question that was wrong. I had asked, "How do you apply this to your life?" This question totally and completely misses the point of the priority of Scripture. We don't apply Scripture to our lives; we apply our lives to Scripture. The Bible and its unmistakable truths were here before we got here, and the Bible and those unmistakable truths will be here after we're gone. The Bible, as the written record of God's activity in and through humankind, is the primary source of all we know to be true about God, redemption, humanity, and everything else that we consider important.

We apply our lives to Scripture. We don't apply Scripture to our lives like we would an acquired skill, like the learning of a new language or time-management skills. We live out or "perform" the eternal truths of the Bible. It's not as if our lives are primary and the Bible is somehow secondary. The Bible and the things of God—those eternal truths—are primary. Our lives are secondary.

> **Scripture is one of God's greatest tools, and with it God seeks to speak truth into our lives.**

Here's how it can be different. If we are serious about wanting to give our kids devotional material, and we are serious about wanting it to be more we-oriented than I-oriented, then here is how we do it. We say, "On this particular date, I want you to read this passage of scripture." In this way we help our teens know what to read, and everybody is on the same page. With this method, we can help our students systematically work through a book of the Bible or through a particular thought process within the Bible.

Now when we say to our group, "Teens, read this scripture," then we must understand that it's also our responsibility to tell them what it means. You might now be saying, "But, Jon, how can I ever be the final authority on the interpretation of Scripture?" Great question. The truth is, none of us will ever get to the place where we can be, in and of ourselves, the final authority on Scripture. However, in order to do our best when asked the tough questions by our teens, we must spend time daily and weekly studying the Scriptures.

I have some reliable books that I reference. I have some people that I reference: people who are smarter than I am, who have studied longer and harder than I have, who are reliable sources of information. When I draw a target on a particular passage, I don't leave that passage until I can make a good faith estimate as to the point that passage of scripture is trying to make. By the time a passage gets to my students, I have lived with it long enough to be able to identify, with conviction, the truth that is being communicated.

Scripture is one of God's greatest tools, and with it God seeks to speak truth into our lives. With it He shapes our perspective, giving us a new pair of glasses through which we can properly see Him, ourselves, and our roles as His people on this planet.

We mentioned earlier in the book that we are living in an age where so many believe themselves to be the final authority on the truth of things. As youth workers, we have a unique and "peculiar" responsibility to guide young minds and hearts through the Word of the Lord—to connect them to a truth that is greater than themselves.

On my new devotional handouts, after helping my teens understand the point of a particular scripture, I now ask them this question: "This being the eternal truth, how will you live out or perform this truth as you live your life this week?"

I hope you can see that this is more than just semantics. I want my teens to see the things of God as primary. I want them to understand that Scripture helps us recognize both God and a godly way of life in the world. I want them to practice rather than just apply. Author Rodney Clapp understands this idea when he writes: "The church does not so much apply Scripture as perform Scripture . . . Scripture really has authority only when it is performed and not merely applied" (Clapp 1996).

Now I know that some of you are reading this and saying to yourself, "Well, that's great for you, Jon. But I just don't have the time to do all of these things." I need to be honest with you. What I'm asking you to do is going to take more of you—more time, more energy, more effort. In fact, it may require that you stop doing some of the things you are now doing, so you can have the time and energy resources to do it. Only as we model worship-centered teaching for our students and provide opportunities for them to join us will they come to understand and find their place in God's Story.

Ideas

Here are some ideas that you can incorporate to begin practicing Worship-centered teaching.

- Try teaching through a narrative book of the Bible—Genesis, Exodus, Esther, the Gospels, Acts, and so on. Teaching through narrative books shows plot lines and character development. You can let the book set the teaching agenda. Let the Scripture teach the lessons it should teach!

- Character sketches—I would recommend that these be done on smaller scales, such as at Bible studies or in small groups. Character sketches can assist us by looking inside the biblical characters that in turn give us insight about ourselves. But, as good as they can be, character sketches are not Scripture. In Scripture, God is the main character, and the people we read about are supporting actors and actresses. In a character sketch, the biblical character plays the leading role.

- Lectionary-based teaching—The lectionary is the work of the Church done hundreds of years ago to organize the reading of Scripture. Traditionally, lectionaries are organized around the Christian calendar. Readings are grouped by particular themes. Most lectionaries are built on a three-year cycle: years A, B, and C. The lectionary can be the source of the sermons and the lessons on any given Sunday. It can also be the source of the daily readings you want to provide for your teens. I have seen lectionaries that contain stories and examples and illustrations that help in the interpretation process. Check out your local Christian bookstore. Go on-line, and look for lectionary-based resources there. One of my favorite web sites is <www.textweek.com>.

- Teach through the Christian calendar—Walk your teens through all of the holidays and symbols found in the Christian calendar.

- Look for curriculum sets that walk you through books of the Bible.

- Provide your teens with Bible reading schedules.

- Ask your teens to rewrite portions of the Bible in their own words. Don't just turn them loose without direction. Let them know that you are going to help them make sure that they get it, that they get the right message across. I recommend rewriting parables, psalms, or proverbs.

- Draw a time line of the biblical stories, and put it up in your youth room.
- Consider buying the book *Spontaneous Melodramas* by Doug Fields, Laurie Polich, and Duffy Robbins. Or write some of your own melodramas.
- Do a series of lessons on Pentecost, Lent, or Advent.
- Study the historic creeds of the Church. Look in your hymnal for copies of the Apostles' Creed and the Nicene Creed.

Reflection Questions

1. Do you know the biblical Story well enough to help your students find their place in it?

2. Does your youth group see themselves as part of the continually unfolding Story? Why or why not?

3. Review the lessons you have taught over the past years. Have you been telling and retelling the Story? Or have you been bouncing from topic to topic? In light of what you have read, what plan do you need to implement to guide your teaching to ensure that you cover the entire Story with your students?

4. Do your lessons give students the opportunity to be actively involved in the learning process?

5. What are some concrete ways that you can begin to change your teaching to reflect a worship-centered teaching approach?

CHAPTER 7

WORSHIP-

CENTERED

COMMUNITY

Telling the Story is just one part of doing worship-centered youth ministry. But telling the Story outside of the community of faith is equivalent to trying to play baseball by yourself. You simply cannot take something that is meant to be done in community and reduce it to an individual activity. Therefore, we will spend this chapter talking about the importance of community in a youth ministry. So, what exactly is worship-centered community?

Worship-Centered Community ...
provides teens with a *means* of *belonging.*

Worship-centered community provides teens with a means of belonging. If you're effective at telling the Story, if you can help teens find their place in God's plan, then you will have given your millennial teen what he or she wants and needs the most—a family with a cause. Do you remember the young man who called himself a "processing member"? He understood there to be a system whereby he would become a fully functional, card-carrying member of the Nation of Islam.

I'm not recommending that we put our students through similar systems before they can belong to our ministries. But the retelling of our Story on a regular basis will give teens a way to belong to God and to His people. They will begin to understand that the Story is still being written by those who participate in it. It will give them regular opportunities to choose to be a part of this family, and over a period of time, they can be initiated and adopted into our family as they align themselves with our distinctive family values and goals.

Having laid claim to our religious and spiritual heritage, they will see us as family—as brothers, sisters, fathers, mothers, sons, and daughters. Jesus himself knew this would happen. In fact, He seems to have indicated that it was to be the norm. Check out Matt. 10:34-39:

> Do not suppose that I have come to bring peace to the earth. I did not come to bring peace, but a sword. For I have come to turn "a man against his father, a daughter against her mother, a daughter-in-law against her mother-in-law—a man's enemies will be the members of his own household." Anyone who loves his father or mother more than me is not worthy of me; anyone who loves his son or daughter more than me is not worthy of me; and anyone who does not take his cross and follow me is not worthy of me. Whoever finds his life will lose it, and whoever loses his life for my sake will find it.

Just as in the Old Testament God established a covenant with Israel, and chose her as His own, so today God establishes His covenant with the Church, the Body of Christ. God intended that our primary family should be the community of faith. As we participate in this community of faith, we begin to understand that our family is much bigger and broader than we could ever have imagined. We realize that it is there that we will find salvation and grace. And as we allow ourselves to participate in the practices that define this family, we begin to reflect to the world what it means to live as a part of the kingdom of God.

Don't get me wrong. I don't mean to insinuate that we are in the business of replacing the "nuclear" family, whatever that means at the dawn of this new millennium. But God makes plain that our allegiance to our human families cannot replace our allegiance to Him and to His family. That allegiance always takes priority.

Worship-Centered Community . . . provides teens with a source of identity and *significance.*

Wrapping our youth into a worship-centered community helps them know what it means to belong to the people of God. And belonging to the people of God means that they have a place within the Story of God. And having a place within the Story of God means that the Story continues to be written through their lives—right here, right now.

Our call is to create a youth ministry that doesn't merely tolerate teens in church, but pours them into the life of the church, so that the church *cannot* go on without them.

Let me ask you a question. Does your church need its teens? If the teens at your church were to be absent on a given Sunday, could you still have church? If the answer is yes, you could have a problem.

How can you measure the strength of a local church youth ministry? If a church is so dependent on its teens that it absolutely could not go on in their absence, that church has not only included its teens but also provided those same teens with a source of identity and significance.

What is it that will give your teens that sense of significance? Knowing that they are needed. What is it that will give your teens a sense of identity? Being active participants in a particular group.

Our challenge is to help our teens see that they are necessary, crucial, essential parts of the church.

Paul understood this when he wrote about the Body of Christ in Rom. 12. Using the analogy of a body, Paul likened each one of us to a body part. Some are the ears, some the nose, some the feet, and some the elbows. And while we may want to give honor only to certain body parts, all parts are equally important to the body.

Paul makes it clear that each of us plays a vital role in the overall health and well-being of the body. Just as a body cannot function without lungs, neither can the church function without its teenagers. Your teens can be, they may even want to be, crucial, essential pieces of all that you do as the Church. They want to take responsibility for their faith, and one of the primary ways they can do this is by becoming active participants in all that happens in their local community of faith.

"But how can my teens be involved in my church?" The better questions may be, "Where can't they be involved?" and "Can our church really afford *not* to commit itself to involving teens in the life and ministry of this church?" With the exception of some of the most priestly work done by the ordained elders in our churches, our teens can and should be involved in any and every aspect of the regularly functioning church.

Do you know any musical teens? Get them up front and involved as soon as possible. Do you know any teens who might be able to help out doing something as simple as greeting or ushering? Press them into service without delay. Are there potential leaders in your group? Begin now to expect leadership from them; put them in places that will require them to exercise their skills for the benefit of their family of faith. Do you know articulate, deep-thinking kids who may already be showing a passion for teaching or preaching? Do your job as a caring youth worker. Talk to your pastor and church leadership and find places of ministry for these young people that will challenge them and sharpen their skills in the process. Your church will benefit from their ministry, and your teens will, at an earlier age, take responsibility for and ownership of their faith.

I happen to believe that this happens easier in smaller churches than it does at our larger megachurches. A friend of mine is a college pastor at a large megachurch. This particular church sits right next to a large Christian university. As you might imagine, a great number of the teens from that local church find their way to the university. Not too long ago, my friend and I were discussing the students that exited "large church" youth ministries and entered college.

It was and continues to be my friend's claim that, by and large, students from smaller churches are the ones who generally are elected to student government offices at the university level and to head ministry teams and organizations. Why? Because they are the ones who were involved in ministry opportunities when they were teens, and have, as a result, developed the skills necessary to be leaders.

The smaller churches have always needed their teens to survive. They are needed to sit in the nursery, to receive the offering, to play the piano, to teach children's Sunday School, to stand in for whoever might be sick, and to clean up after the service. As a result, they grow up understanding that to be identified with a group of people is to be actively involved in the whole life of that group of people.

Our challenge, if we are all to create worship-centered community, is to help our teens see that they are necessary, crucial, essential parts of the church. And while that may be a greater challenge at a larger church, it is no less crucial. The challenge for all of us, whether we are the youth pastor of a megachurch or a youth worker at a little church, is to find places of effective, meaningful involvement for our teens. When we do this, our teens will naturally find their identity as the people of God.

Worship-Centered Community ... provides teens with a place to discover *truth* and define *values.*

We've talked about it before, and this is the perfect place to revisit it. Belonging precedes value formation. More than ever before we need to let kids know, "This is what we believe." "This is what the church believes." Because teens want to belong and they're ready (in a worship-driven community) to adjust their individual values to match a group's values, we must take advantage. We need to show them True North—the God of the Story, a Story best told by a biblically functioning community.

Never apologize for the high values of the church. Don't be afraid to articulate what the worshiping community believes to be the truth about a particular subject, but do your homework first. Remember, our job is not to convince our teens that other beliefs are wrong. Instead we need to simply say, "This is what we believe. This is who we are."

I want to tell you a story about Christie. I met Christie in the fall of 1997 while volunteering at the alternative high school I've previously mentioned. If you're not familiar with alternative schools, then know that this school is where students are sent when they can't or won't fit into the mainstream classroom. Violence problems, substance abuse problems, teenage moms, students with mild learning or attention deficit disorders— these are the type of students you'll find at this school. When I met Christie, she was beginning what was supposed to be her sophomore year. It was supposed to be her sophomore year, but she had been gone for so much of her freshman year while in substance abuse programs that she was repeating that year instead.

The first time I saw Christie, she was the picture of rage—the dark, baggy clothes; the long, stringy hair; the massive leather jacket; the illegal chains hanging out of her pockets. I know you can't judge a book by its cover, but this was more than an "outfit" Christie had on. She admitted that this look was a statement.

This was probably the single angriest kid I had ever seen in my entire life; and why not? To say that Christie was from a broken home is a severe understatement. Her homelife was more than broken; it was demolished. She had never lived at one address for more than a year and a half in her entire life, and she spent at least a portion of that life being passed back and forth between feuding parents. She had every right to be angry.

God directed me to invest myself in Christie. I enlisted the help of my family of faith, and over the course of weeks and months, a friendship was begun. Please know that this wasn't just me; it was my wife, the compassionate one; it was Lee, our middle school pastor; it was others on my youth staff; it was several of our teens, and many others of our church family. We all worked together as one to reach out to Christie.

Over a period of time, we convinced Christie that she was worth liking and loving. It did not happen quickly. We first discovered Christie in the middle of the fall semester, and it probably was the middle of the spring before we could convince her to show up at the church, and even then, her coming was not so much out of her own spiritual curiosity as much as it was to be with those of us willing to be known as her friends.

Please understand that at this point in her "journey," Christie was not what most of us would call a Christian. She was not a believer; her life reflected no heart commitment, but the attractiveness of our family of faith was beginning to make her aware of what she wasn't. She started to notice some of these things that she didn't have but needed.

It was during the fall semester of her junior year, while she was living with her father in Midwest City (a suburb of Oklahoma City, about 30 minutes east of the church), that Christie made the decision to subject and submit her life story to the continuing Story of God and His people. We had been talking about all that God would want to do for her, in her, and with her, if given the opportunity. My wife and I had been so careful not to leverage or intimidate Christie to a place of decision. Christie was much too stubborn to ever be pressured into anything. Christie wasn't leveraged into the faith; she was romanced into the faith by God as He worked through His people at our church. Christie had come to faith by watching the family of God behave like a family. "And the Lord added to their number daily those who were being saved" (Acts 2:47). Christie had now willingly entered into the process of being initiated, even adopted into God's family. She was now an initiate into this community of faith.

Now I would like to tell you that things changed radically and quickly for Christie, but in all reality, that simply wasn't the case. To be honest, Christie was still struggling with a drug problem. She desperately wanted to quit, but her immediate family opted not to help—they had their own problems. Her dad sat her down on the bed and said, "Christie, we are rooting for you! We want you to be able to break free from drugs, but you need to know something. I have chosen a lifestyle that includes drugs. I can handle it, and I am going to keep doing it."

Because she knew she wouldn't be able to quit, she moved out of her dad's house with his complete blessing. She moved in with her mother who, like her father, had chosen a lifestyle that she didn't want to give up. And Christie, who was being shaped by the Story of God and His people, began to realize that if she was going to overcome this drug problem, she was going to have to move again.

Over a period of time, she had come to the awareness through her participation in the community of faith that it was not OK for a member of the family of God to do pot, that it was not OK for a member of the family of God to drink to the point of alcoholism. And don't for one minute believe that her decisions to move out and away from her mom and dad were somehow demonstrative of a lack of care and concern for her own family. Nothing could be farther from the truth. In fact, Christie's decisions to separate herself were made for the benefit of her family. It was and continues to be Christie's dream that one day she could be involved in the reclamation of her own family.

In the meantime, Christie continued to be formed into the family of God. A godly family in our church recognized Christie's need for a place to live, opened their doors, and Christie moved in and stayed for the remainder of her high school days.

One Sunday, Christie noticed an announcement aimed at all who were interested in being baptized. She brought the announcement to me and asked for an explanation. "What is baptism?" she asked. "What does it mean?"

"It is a public proclamation, a public testimony," I answered. "It is both your public statement of faith and a ritual whereby you are 'initiated'—in an official way—into this family of faith."

She said, "I think I'm ready for all of that now." Christie correctly had the impression that this was a pretty monumental decision that she was about to make—the kind you want your family to see. So she called her dad and her mom and said, "I'm going to get baptized on Sunday night, and I would like for you to be there." They both agreed, but then on the day of the ceremony, both of them called and said they weren't coming.

Christie was crushed. As the one who does much of the baptizing at our church, I'm not used to seeing baptism candidates with such long faces. She attended the preservice baptism candidates' meeting and never cracked a grin. After the meeting, I took her aside and I said to her, "This is supposed to be a pretty good day for you. Do you want to wait to be baptized?"

"No," she replied, "I'm ready."

I baptized Christie that night. After the ceremony, she got dried off and went home without a word. I remember feeling these strange contradictory emotions that night. On the one hand, I rejoiced in Christie's public testimony. But on the other hand, I agonized over Christie's loneliness. I have to admit that I felt more defeated than I did anything else.

But I will never forget what happened the next day. After school, Christie rolled into the parking lot and walked into the church with a recognizable spring in her step. She walked into our offices, and said, "I know you all could tell that I was pretty disappointed last night when my family couldn't be there. But then it hit me—my family was there."

Do you get it? We are not in the business of breaking up family. We are still trying to lead both her mom and her dad to Christ. But we absolutely are in the business of being family for those who belong to our fellowship. Just to bring you up to speed, Christie graduated from high school and entered Southern Nazarene University as 1 of 30 students selected to receive a ministerial scholarship. Her life has been spoken for, as she feels called to work with at-risk teens.

It can happen! Sure, it takes weeks and months and years, and we don't really think we have that kind of time to wait on results—to determine whether we have been successful. And the truth is, you and I by ourselves don't have that kind of time. But we have to remember that this is not an individual enterprise. It takes the entire community of faith working together to make stories like Christie's happen. As the Church tells and retells its Story, as the Church allows its identity and priorities to be shaped by the God of the Story, and as the Church lives like family, then and only then will the family of God be attractive enough to compel people like Christie to want to belong, to want to build relationships, and finally, to want to be adopted as a son or daughter.

Ideas

People often ask, "How can I develop a worship-centered community in my ministry to teens?" Most of us who have spent any time at all in youth ministry have yearned for our teens to sense some kind of unity. I'm hoping for something more than just unity; I'm hoping for "community." But how will you build that sense of family-with-a-purpose into your teens? Let's talk ideas.

First, let me say this: worship-centered community takes time. It is not yet in pill form, so you will have to be patient. Worship-centered community is built a layer at a time as we tell and retell the Story, and as relationships between people are started and then strengthened. In this age of the microwave, think of these ideas as Crock-Pot youth ministry.

The ideas I have for you below are divided into four categories. Keep in mind that these are just some ideas that I have found helpful. I fully expect that you will have other and better ideas that will be appropriate for your situation. Use what you can, and allow the rest to stimulate your own thinking in this area.

1. To build better worship-centered community, learn to *serve together.*
   - Mission trips can be great community-building experiences, but you don't have to go for a week and you don't have to go out of the state. In fact, if you will figure out a way to work service into the regular function of your youth ministry, then those teens who go and serve together not only will be doing hands-on ministry (one of the most effective teaching tools) but also will begin to feel a belonging and a unity that other teens who can't or won't participate, won't feel.

     "Hit and run" mission experiences will only provide limited help for you and your teens. Identity is shaped in the regular commitment to service. Work in the soup lines on a regular basis; do fewer activities in a month and work more often at the city mission.

- Challenge your teens to be regularly involved in the function of the church. You've heard the slogan "Membership has its privileges." Make sure your teens also understand that membership has its responsibilities. Help your church learn to depend on its teens. And help your teens understand that when they work together in the church, they can accomplish great things for God.

2. To build better worship-centered community, learn to *reach together.*
   - Assist your teens in learning how to build relationships with those teens who are not yet in your church and with those teens who have stopped coming to your church. Not all of my teens helped reclaim Christie. But those who did join me in that process experienced greater community.
   - Encourage your teens to develop a system whereby a newcomer can begin the process of being adopted into the group.
   - Encourage your teens to visit newcomers.
   - Encourage your teens to write notes to newcomers or to teens who have stopped coming. (By the way, I'm not talking about stealing teens from other churches; that *completely* misses the point.)
   - Encourage your teens to call newcomers or those teens who seem to have fallen through the cracks.

3. To build better worship-centered community, find time to *be together.*
   - Small(er) Groups—This itch to belong that teens are feeling will not be scratched when that teen is 1 of 50, or 1 of 25, or even 1 of 10. You need to break your group down to groups of 4 to 5, groups small enough for a person to know and be known by the other people in the group. That being said, I don't pretend to know your program well enough to tell you how to tailor it or how to alter it. I just know that in order to build worship-centered community, somehow, someway, you have to make a big group small. But keep this in mind: these groups will be relational groups, groups of friends. That being the case, please, please don't try to "assign" groups, and stop trying to explode

the "cliques" in your group. The decision to open up a group like that will have to come from the inside; you can't force it and hope that anyone will benefit by it. Concepts like accountability and confession and vulnerability—all incredible, community-building tools—require the kind of trust that comes as a result of companionship. Instead of exploding the differing groups, find ways for them to partner and interact. Community happens as we find common ground.

- Champion the cause of being together. Find ways for your teens to hang out together. There is no substitute for time spent with friends.
- Eat together.
- Interconnect your teens. Make contact information (especially E-mail addresses) available to all of those involved in your ministry.

4. To build better worship-centered community, *share common experiences.* You've no doubt heard the saying "The family that prays together, stays together." We're trying to build family here. So praying together will help us too! In fact, look at this: "The family that _____ together, stays together." The next time you're hurting for a community-building idea, be creative and fill in the blank. Keep your goals in mind, and you'll be amazed at the things you can do to build community. Such as:

- Play together.
- Travel. Take long bus trips together.
- Camp out.
- Ropes course.
- Take pictures. It seems like every time I get kids together, I have to tell someone at some point to put the pictures away, because they just love looking at themselves in pictures. Pictures tell stories.
- Develop pictures. This is where I struggle. How many of you have rolls of undeveloped, unidentifiable film in your office? You're almost afraid to develop them.
- Post the pictures. What if you built your own youth ministry

time line along one of the walls in your youth room? Fall retreat. Spring retreat. Disciple Now. Summer camp. Mission
trip. Your teens will walk up to those pictures and immediately
say, "Do you remember when . . . ?" And they will start telling
the stories that have made and are making your group into an
attractive community that people will want to belong to.

Reflection Questions

1. How good is your youth ministry and church at being family to the teens
   that you minister to?

2. Does your local church look on youth ministry as an adolescent baby-sit-
   ting service, or do they view the teens in your church as a resource to be
   utilized? If the former, why?

3. How involved are the teens in your ministry in the life of the whole
   church? Would your church function as normal if the teens didn't show
   up?

4. What are some of the ways that your church helps to initiate teens into
   the faith?

5. What are some concrete things that your church can do to become a
   worship-centered community?

CHAPTER 8

WORSHIP-

CENTERED

REFLECTION

Once youth have grounded their identity in the Story of God and once they feel they are part of the community of faith, is that the end? What is the next step in worship-centered youth ministry? The answer: worship-centered reflection.

The choice of the word *reflection* was a difficult one for me. I was looking for the perfect word that would communicate informed action, practice, and participation. I considered words like *action, response,* and even *life,* but I just couldn't get comfortable with any of them. I settled on the word *reflection* because it can have two meanings, and I like both. Let me try to explain it to you with one more story.

Meaning No. 1 — To ponder . . .

Last fall I bit the bullet and dedicated my Wednesday night teaching times to the retelling of our biblical Story. For 30 weeks I tracked through those stories most responsible for defining us as a people, the people of God. We started at the beginning and tracked all the way through to Pentecost. We told the stories of Paul's missionary journeys, and then we concluded the biblical part of our time line with a lesson on the hope of the Second Coming. I had commissioned two of my youth staff workers to generate for us a massive time line — one big enough to show each of the stories we had retold during the year and still leave several feet of blank space between Pentecost and the Second Coming.

I said to my teens, "This is the Story of God's interaction with His people, our ancestors. It's our Story. It's a Story that continues to be written in the hearts and lives of those who are willing to submit their life stories to His Story. You see all of this blank space here between Pentecost and the Second Coming? Your face, your picture, your Story can belong here. Mine can too. If we are willing, like so many of these men and women who have gone before us, to commit our lives to something bigger than ourselves, to the continued writing of this Story, then we, too, have a place on this time line."

By this time my youth staff were armed with Polaroid cameras. As students came to the front, their smiling faces were photographed and then taped on this time line. This was a truly meaningful time for all involved.

Reflecting on the Story moves people to a point of decision. Thankfully, that night many of my teens (but not all) decided to make public their decision to belong to the Story that continues to be written.

Meaning No. 2 — To project an image . . .

As great as that night was, I knew that my work was really just beginning. As their pastor and shepherd, I had fulfilled my responsibility to retell the Story. But now we faced the responsibility to keep in front of our teens an understanding of the responsibilities that go along with being the people of God.

Being the people of God means committing to be a part of whatever it is that God is doing. You do realize that God is up to something, don't you? The biblical Story is the best evidence we have of how God has worked in the past. And with it we can connect the dots, not just to map where we have come from but also to give us some understanding as to where we are going.

Do you see where God is at work today? To recognize this, we have to see things the way God sees things. This happens as the Story shapes our lives. We begin to change, seeking to fit our lives into God's plan and purpose. We desperately desire to be used by God and so we seek to find where God is at work.

The truth is, God is at work everywhere we look, if we look with spiritual eyes. He is the teen serving at a soup kitchen for homeless people. He is the youth worker seeking to befriend a teenager. He is the family giving up a week of vacation so they can send money to feed starving children in Africa.

The people of God are set apart by God for a particular purpose—the redemption of the planet! As the Church, we are God's chosen instruments whereby He moves and works and redeems more and more of creation back to himself.

That being the case, nothing is more tragic than the church that exists only for itself—the youth ministry that exists to keep its teens off the streets and entertained. Archbishop William Temple, as quoted by John Stott, may best describe the purpose of the church when he says, "The church is the only co-operative society in the world which exists for the benefit of its nonmembers" (Stott 1992). Does that statement capture your church and your ministry to teens? Or are you chronically normal? Does your budget reflect your priority schedule? How much time and energy and money do you spend to see to it that your teens have a great time? How much of your time and energy and money do you spend to reach those outside the church?

The dramatic and accurate retelling of the biblical Story will absolutely and necessarily reveal the priorities and intentions of God. And at the point that we choose to claim that Story as our own, then God's priorities and intentions become our priorities and intentions. When we do this thing right, we *reflect* God's heart: His belief in and passion for people of every kind; His never ending optimism that all can be reached; His concern for social justice; His hunger for peace; His love of a good time; even His care and concern for the environment.

The more the church focuses solely on it own members, the more we miss the point and the more we fail to meet our obligation as the people of God.

You have the cure for what is ailing all of creation. What will you do with it?

> The more the church focuses solely on its own members, the more we miss the point and the more we fail to meet our obligation as the people of God.

Worship-Centered Reflection . . . has a ministry mind-set.

I like the trend away from using the term *youth group* and toward the term *youth ministry.* It has the right heart. It is at least the beginning of the understanding that we are here to do what God is doing.

Youth worker, I know you face pressure to entertain, to keep your teens occupied. I know that you have parents who still consider you to be a cheap, trusted, wholesome baby-sitter. I know, too, that your pastor or church leaders may be asking you to fulfill a role that makes you look more like an activities director on a cruise ship and less like the shepherd your teens really need you to be. It may even be that you've found yourself in a church whose youth ministry traditions have been set for many years, and you may have very few choices when it comes to budgeting and pro-gramming. And you still face the very real possibility that your teens may "vote with their feet," and abandon this worship-centered, ministry-ori-ented approach for other youth programs that only offer games and fun. You face the pressure to be everything but the real Church.

Any or all of those things may be true, but the God of the Story asks you, as His handpicked representative, to lead His people toward Him and away from themselves, and trust me, He knows what the costs will be.

Your teens' ability to involve themselves in the Story may be largely dependent on your ability to redefine the purpose and practice of youth ministry. What are you doing on a regular basis to provide opportunities for your teens to be meaningfully and routinely involved in ministry?

Earlier we claimed identity and significance as two of the benefits of worship-centered community. We made the statement, "Your church needs to need its teens." We encouraged you to find ways to incorporate them into places of significant responsibility. The benefits are significant, but equally significant are the risks of *not* doing the things we mentioned above. Your teens are already in danger of missing the point if faith has been defined in such a way as to allow them to be passive recipients of all that the church has to offer.

Your church isn't a cruise ship. The church doesn't exist for its peo-ple; the people exist for the church—to help the church be the redemptive tool in the hands of God! Rather than a cruise ship, your church is one of those old massive ships with no motor, but hundreds of oars. If you are adopting a ministry mind-set as part of your worship-centered youth ministry, everyone gets an oar because everyone knows that rowing is a natural and expected part of being on the ship.

Worship-centered youth ministry that has a ministry mind-set defines faith in such a way that it invites involvement into the grand scheme of things.

Worship-Centered Reflection . . . has a missions mind-set.

This particular subject merited its own section, not because it is radically different from the things that have already been said, but because of an alarming trend in youth "missions."

I am a big fan of the well-designed mission trip. I myself have seen lives altered because of these types of experiences. But I am thoroughly frightened and disgusted by those "mission" events that are little more than vacations with detours.

We must diligently defend against the underdefining of mission or compassion. We can't allow our teens to understand missions as something you do somewhere else for one or two weeks out of the year. At that point, mission work is just something a person does to ease his or her conscience or to put something on a résumé or just to get away and get to a beach.

None of these are compassion. Broken into its parts, the word *compassion* literally means "to suffer with." Henri Nouwen, in his book *Compassion,* wonders out loud if it's really compassion when your plane ticket back home is in your pocket (Nouwen 1982).

It's so easy to miss the point. Missions and compassionate ministries aren't about us! It's not about the people doing the ministering; it's about the people in pain. We don't do these things in order to be better, more spiritual people. When that is our mind-set, we are doing nothing more than patronizing those to whom we minister. Rather than seeing them as people of worth, we instead look down our noses at "these poor people." And when we get home, our teens testify, "Everything that I saw made me so appreciative of all that God has given to me." Gratitude is great, but if in our missions efforts our teens don't look into the eyes of people and see them as worthy of sacrifice as themselves, if they don't "participate" in suffering and empathize with those to whom they are ministering, then they have missed the point, and we have missed an opportunity to retell the Story.

Worship-centered youth ministry that has a missions mind-set happens not because the missionary needs to do it in order to be a missionary but because, as a missionary, it is the only way he or she knows to live.

As our teens participate in the Story and in God's grand design, their sense of corporate identity as missionaries will work itself out wherever they happen to be.

A missions-oriented mind-set means that we will practice social justice. Believers need to take stands against such issues as prejudice, poverty, exploitation, and violence. To this point, the millennial generation seems to have strong opinions on society and societal ills.

We can't afford to allow missions work to be seen as something that happens one week a year, in a place other than home. To the contrary, as our teens participate in the Story and in God's grand design, their sense of corporate identity as missionaries will work itself out wherever they happen to be.

Consider the parable of the Good Samaritan found in Luke 10. The entire parable is Jesus' answer to a Jewish theologian's question, "What must I do to inherit eternal life?"

Jesus answers the question with a question, "You're the expert in the Law of God. What do you think?"

The old man answered, "Love God, and love your *neighbor* as yourself."

"Do this and you will live," Jesus replied.

But the Jewish teacher of the Law wasn't satisfied yet. "Who is my neighbor?" he asked.

Jesus answered with the parable of the Good Samaritan, in which a hated Samaritan played the role of hero while a priest and a Levite played the roles of the fools. In Jesus' example, only the Samaritan fulfilled Jesus' definition of a good neighbor. How? By seeing himself as a tool in God's hands for the meeting of human need. The Samaritan man didn't stop and help so that he could testify in his Samaritan church later that night. He didn't stop and help because it was his week of the year to help. He didn't stop because of a promise of a two-night stay in a nice hotel by the beach after the work was completed. He stopped because he understood himself to be a neighbor to another human being, to any human being.

May this parable define and describe our missionary journeys as well.

Worship-Centered Reflection . . . expresses itself in our play.

Play is any activity that celebrates God's connections with His people, and His peoples' connections with each other. You'll need to keep that definition around for reference's sake.

We shoot ourselves in the foot if we take away fun and games from our teens. Today's teens are forced to bear the brunt of growing up too fast and too soon, and we need to create an environment where teens can enjoy the freedom and joy that comes only from being involved in the family of God.

Rather than giving you an argument behind worship-centered play, I just want to describe it.

1. It is a contagious *outbreak* of fun!

I have to constantly remind myself that fun for teens is probably different from fun for me. Fun for me may be having a Coke and reading a good book. Fun for a teen might be seeing how fast he or she can rip up a book and shove it into a large pop bottle.

Here are a couple of things we should remember about fun.

A. Simple things work best.

Play, by definition, is highly relational. It is often what we like to call "a contagious outbreak of fun."

Here's what I mean. Many of you will be able to identify with the horror story known as a junior high boys' lock-in. Our church had one scheduled. I didn't even have to be there. I was just doing my friend, the junior high pastor, a favor. I guess I had some sort of death wish or something. When we have a lock-in, we don't just go and stay in one place; we move around going from place to place, trying to fight off sleep. We start out at the church and we end up at the church, but in between, we are everywhere else.

Now, if you have been doing lock-ins for any length of time at all, you know the window of danger. It's from somewhere around two o'clock to four o'clock in the morning when things can go either way. It can either get violent and ugly as people (especially the adults) decide that sleep is the better option, or you can find something fun and entertaining enough to pacify tired minds and bodies until morning.

Well, we had done a couple of things, but we were reaching the danger point. It was in the middle of the summer, and it was plenty warm to go swimming. We drove the short distance to the pool; it was two o'clock in the morning, the hour of truth. We put our suits on, walked to the pool, and the unthinkable happened. There was silence and no swimming. I said to our junior high pastor, "It's happened. We've got trouble."

Also present that night was Jeff, a youth worker of significant stature and a dangerously creative mind. Jeff could sense the danger we were now in. So he made an executive decision.

He looked over in the corner and there was one of those light plastic, multicolored balls you can get at any self-respecting supermarket for 99 cents. He walked over and picked up this ball and looked at one of the eighth grade studs. He got about six or seven feet behind him, reared back, and with everything that he had, just pounded that teen in the back of the head. There was a stunned silence until Jeff roared with laughter and jumped in the pool. That eighth grade stud rubbed the back of his head, smiled, and picked up the ball. Suddenly he fired the ball at an unsuspecting seventh grader, and then he jumped in the pool. This happened over and over until every person was in the pool, struggling for control of one of these heat-seeking missiles.

This went on for an hour and a half—25 boys and a couple of sponsors just nailing one another with those balls. As the night dragged on, they named this game and drew up a few rules. They even figured out a way to crown a winner! If you were to ask those guys after the lock-in which part was the most fun, it wouldn't have been the bowling, the carpet golf, or the late, late movie—it was that stupid game. Now, why was that game so impacting and so fun? Well, because it was highly relational. It was simple enough to be relational.

B. Be creative!

Remember we are working with the "been there, done that" generation. We will have to dig down and stir up the creative juices to come up with a new generation of fun. Think of things never done before, go to weird places, try strange things. Keep up the search for new and effective ideas, but don't forget to look within—you are your greatest source of ideas.

2. It builds up and doesn't tear down.

A. Emphasize community.

Beware of the games that celebrate the fittest—the best athlete, the fastest, the biggest, the strongest. Beware of games that judge or label the loser. Beware of games that single out students and make them look silly or stupid. Nothing can destroy a developing relationship quicker. Yet far too many games books are chock-full of these types of games.

Instead, play games that emphasize the community. Try to play games that are we-oriented, where everyone gets to participate. Try to play games where being the winner isn't as important as the fact that you played. Playing these types of games will help strengthen relationships as students and sponsors laugh and play together.

B. Don't take safety lightly.

Don't take safety lightly. This is important, and it may be most important to the parents. You're going to have a hard time convincing a parent that you have a teen's spiritual best at heart when you don't have that teen's physical best at heart. And remember this: a teen that doesn't feel safe in your group will not be free to grow spiritually.

3. It has a purpose.

We are trying to do something with these playtimes. So, it might require you to do some advance thinking and working. A good game might be the perfect way to illustrate the point you are trying to make in a given teaching time.

For example, recently I was trying to help my teens understand the importance of growing in faith. "Don't stay where you are!" I said. "Make plans and preparations to grow!" I happened to be working through the Book of Luke, and this night we were working our way through the 14th chapter. We read the passage of scripture about the man who planned to build the tower. "Suppose one of you wants to build a tower. Will he not first sit down and estimate the cost to see if he has enough money to complete it? For if he lays the foundation and is not able to finish it, everyone who sees it will ridicule him, saying, 'This fellow began to build and was not able to finish'" (vv. 28-30).

I immediately divided my group into five groups; I tossed each group a bag of 50 balloons and a roll of Scotch tape. I said to them, "The group with the tallest, free-standing structure wins. You've got 10 minutes. Go!"

A mad rush of activity ensued for the following 10 minutes. Groups organized themselves, and soon the towers were taking shape. After 10 minutes were up, we crowned a winner, and I immediately started asking questions.

"What's the point? What did you learn in playing this game?" Not surprisingly (for I have brilliant children), they had all the right answers. Listen to what they learned.

"Spiritual growth doesn't just happen. We have to be smart about it, like the builder who wants to build a tower, like the general who goes out to fight a war."

"Spiritual growth is intentional. There are some things you need to do, some plans you need to make."

"There are a lot of people involved in building a tower of faith."

Youth worker, you've got to try this stuff. Your teens will enjoy it, they will "get" the point you are trying to make, and they will think you are a genius.

But make no mistake. This kind of intentionality will require you to establish some criteria and goals for your time at play. It will require you to stay focused on your criteria and goals even and especially when your teens have other ideas.

Ideas

How can I do worship-centered reflection?

1. Have a ministry mind-set.
   - Define Christianity in such a way as to include an emphasis on reinvesting oneself in the Church.
   - Encourage your teens to exercise their musical talents in church *on a regular basis.*
   - Encourage your teens to assist the children's workers *on a regular basis.*

- Train teens to be ushers, greeters, and parking attendants.
- If you have a youth council, make sure that you have a teen in charge of, or at least involved in, the seeking out of ministry opportunities in the church.
- If you're not already doing it, make sure that everyone knows that you will be eliminating one activity a month to make room for more ministry involvement.

2. Have a missions mind-set.
   - Seek out mission opportunities that exist in your neighborhood, and clear out time in your youth calendar so that you and your teens can be involved in the meeting of human needs *on a regular basis*.
   - Participate in a nonviolent demonstration against some form of social injustice.
   - Recycle.
   - Regularly gather food and clothes to contribute to the local shelters.
   - Ask your teens to volunteer their time to the elderly or handicapped. (One of my teens goes on a weekly basis to read to a little girl with cerebral palsy.)
   - Do a fund-raiser to raise money for the poor.
   - Participate in "World Feast" (contact them at 1-816-333-7000, ext. 2215, or write: YouthServe, 6401 The Paseo, Kansas City, MO 64131) or The 30 Hour Famine (contact them at 1-800-7-FAMINE or on the Web at <www.30hourfamine.org>). Both of these events allow your teens to raise money for starving kids around the world.

3. Make time for play.
   - Ropes courses
   - Camp-outs
   - Outdoor, high-impact activities
   - Team sports
   - Games that teach (like the balloon castles activity previously mentioned)

Reflection Questions

1. Why is it so important to think theologically (to reflect) about youth ministry?

2. In what ways does your youth ministry promote service and missions?

3. Do you ever purposely make time for play in your youth ministry? Why should play be such an important part of our ministry to youth?

4. What are some concrete ways that you can be more intentional about having a ministry mind-set? having a missions mind-set? making time for play?

CHAPTER 9

THE ROLE OF THE WORSHIP-CENTERED YOUTH WORKER

We started this book off with a confession or two. We might as well finish with one.

I've used the term *worship-centered* to get your attention.

Worship, as in "praise and worship," is a movement of epidemic proportions. It has become a singular focus for many believers and many congregations, so much so that for many the focus is no longer the worship of God but the worship of worship, or as Moses himself might describe it, idolatry.

We have "progressed" or "grown" to the point that we now underdefine, and as a result underappreciate, what it means to be a people of worship. So I have used the hottest of the modern-day hot buttons to bring attention to what I believe to be one of the greatest dangers facing the people of God.

Don't misunderstand. I haven't misrepresented myself or Scripture. As a matter of fact, I have only mentioned a few of the passages in the Bible that seem to indicate a connectedness between an understanding of God's Story (as found in the Bible), and God's peoples' understanding of issues of identity, community, and responsibility (answering questions like "Who are we?" "Where do we belong?" "What do we do now?"). Let's look together at a few right now.

- Deut. 6 — The Shema, the charge to retell the Story to future generations.
- Josh. 24 — At Shechem, Joshua challenges the people of Israel to fidelity.
- The Story is invoked each and every time Yahweh is labeled as the God of Abraham, Isaac, and Jacob.
- Salvation history psalms (such as 105 and 106) — Psalms used in liturgy to remind God's people of His actions in history.
- Neh. 9 — 10 — The Story is retold at the rededication of the rebuilt wall for the purpose of encouraging Israel's fidelity.
- Matt. 1 — The genealogy of Jesus. An account of the history of the people of Israel that would eventuate in the birth of the Messiah.
- The entire Book of Matthew is written in an attempt to reveal Christ's connectedness with the God and the Story of the Old Testament.
- Acts 7 — Stephen's speech to the Sanhedrin is a recounting of the Story, meant to demonstrate how far Israel had deviated from God's design.

This is by no means meant to be an exhaustive listing. It is merely a taste of the Bible's understanding why it is important to tell and retell the Story. Scripture is shot through with sometimes spoken and sometimes unspoken knowledge of a moving plotline. God is up to something. He has always been up to something, namely the redemption of all creation, and the Bible is the record of God's progressive activity in human history.

It is the task of today's Church to help its people know the dream of God, *and* to know how and where believers can participate in the here and coming Kingdom.

But there is another term that describes the mind-set I have written about in this book. It is a term that has become increasingly credible and popular in recent decades, so popular that many of you have been waiting for me to use it for about 100 pages now. OK, here it is—the term is *narrative theology*. In his book *The Story of God,* Michael Lodahl defines narrative theology as a method that is "attentive to the biblical story, especially as it impinges upon and even profoundly shapes our own individual stories" (Lodahl 1994).

What a perfect definition! In other words, narrative theology understands that the biblical narrative actively seeks to shape our individual stories; it intends to weave us into its ever-unfolding plot.

In this book we have described an overarching operating system, all the way down to your group games. But what is the role of the worship-centered youth worker? How can you as a youth worker most effectively tell this Story and "do" narrative theology?

In his book *The Wounded Healer,* Henri Nouwen tells the story of being the chaplain on a cruise ship. On its way into port, the ship ran into fog so thick that the steersman couldn't see his own bow. The captain was understandably and visibly nervous as he paced back and forth across the deck, poring over radio transmissions on the whereabouts of other ships in the area. On one of his trips across the deck, he ran into Nouwen. Frustrated, the captain barked at Nouwen and ordered him to stay out of the way. Nouwen, embarrassed, insulted, and emotionally wounded, turned to walk away when the captain shouted back, "Why don't you stay around. This might be the only time I really need you" (Nouwen 1972).

As Nouwen relates the story, he wonders out loud if his experience on the deck of this ship is symbolic of the attitude our society has for churches and for ministers in general. No doubt he knows the answer. As I have previously stated, the church is in great danger of not being noticed anymore. And I will say it again: being ignored is much worse than being hated. Knowing this, the Church has continually worked to maintain its popularity, often at the cost of its peculiarity.

And sadly, there are too many youth workers out there who are more concerned with popularity than with peculiarity. You've seen them. They're the ones who equate success with busyness. They're the ones whose ministry calendars betray a commitment to the entertainment of teens and not to their initiation or adoption into the Story. They're the ones whose families are sacrificed on the altar of "church work." They're the ones who are burning out at an alarming rate because they are spending so much more than they are taking in. And if they're not burning out, these are the men and women who are moving to a new assignment once every two to three years because they have exhausted their supply of material.

These are the youth workers who have no real focus, scrambling from week to week to put together some sort of program. They are, in essence, putting Band-Aids on cancerous wounds rather than focusing on the real disease. They can't help millennial teens find their places in the Story because the youth workers don't know the Story themselves. They don't know how to tell the Story, and consequently, they haven't found their own place in the Story.

Youth worker, you're asked to wear several hats—calendar coordinator, best friend, spiritual leader, praise and worship leader, orator, visionary, and "life of the party"—not to mention husband or wife and father or mother.

Give it up. You can't do it all, and what's more, you're not supposed to.

You run yourself ragged, wear yourself out, and here's the worst part, you abdicate your God-given role to be a minister to youths. You become the useless chaplain on the cruise ship whose presence is only really needed when danger is imminent.

If I may, please allow me get personal for a moment with those of you reading this book who are professional youth pastors. There's something we need to understand about our role. Simply put, we have been called to be ministers to our teens, and we should act like ministers. Please don't misunderstand me. I'm not saying that there are roles that are "beneath" us. I'm simply reminding us that if we are going to do the work of being a minister, there are certain things that we will be asked to do that should be done by others in our faith communities. When we, the ministers, are trapped doing things like planning the next afterglow or amusement park day, then we will not have the time or the energy to do and be what God wants us to do and be for the benefit of His people.

All of us, whether we are professional youth workers or volunteers, are

God's representatives to tell and then to interpret God's Story for those entrusted to our care. We are the ones to whom is given the task of telling the Story. We are the ones asked to connect the dots. We are the ones who (maybe even literally) draw the time line of God's interaction with human history. And it's we who help young people learn to subject their individual stories to the dreams of God for the world. Please understand, you are absolutely crucial to the process of narrative theology.

Yes, I know. I've heard and read all of the same things you have about the dreaded "Messiah complex" suffered by those who mistakenly place themselves in the center instead of God. But we have now reached the place where the Church can and must reintroduce itself as the people of God. The people of God have always been dependent on those who would allow themselves to be used by God to tell and interpret the Story.

You and I are navigators. Yes, you and I, the one with no sense of geographical direction at all. We are called by God to guide and direct our teens through the stormy seas of life.

How will we do it?

> **We are called by God to guide and direct our teens through the stormy seas of life.**

Step No. 1—Learn the Story

First and foremost, we commit to God and His dream by recommitting ourselves to the understanding of the biblical Story. How well do you know the Story? Have you read all the way through your Bible, or has someone convinced you that there are parts that aren't worth your time? Do you know the books of the Bible? Could you construct a time line that would include 10 to 12 of the most important, history-shaping people of God-shaping events?

Believers, it is not enough to simply read Scripture. What is the use in reading it if you don't or won't understand it? As you read Scripture, you need to know how a particular story fits into the overall message and movement of the plot.

Before we can begin to communicate this Story and call students to belong, we have to learn to appreciate the Bible's interconnectedness. We have to be able to see the movement, to connect the dots, and to plot the direction that God is moving in and through His people, the Church. Being a good navigator is dependent upon knowing the terrain (life) and having a map (Scripture) to guide us.

Step No. 2—Tell the Story

This is more than a matter of teaching. In this book we have talked about the importance of telling the Story in order to help our teens understand themselves as a community or family and how to demonstrate our identity and commitment to God's dream. As we practice being the people of God, telling the Story will be a natural part of who we are.

Francis of Assisi is famous for having said, "Preach the Gospel at all times; if necessary, use words." In the same way, we need to make sure that everything we do, both the spoken areas and the unspoken areas, points in the same navigational direction. Avoid anything and everything that doesn't move you and your teens in the right direction. You don't have time to waste. You don't have the luxury of meaningless activity.

One of our most effective teaching examples will be the way in which we live our own lives. What does our devotional life say about our relationship with God? What does our relationship with our family teach? And (this is huge) how do we filter through everything that is vying for our time and attention and focus on the most important things in life? How do we react and respond to the inevitable pains of life?

Stay the course. Resist the temptation to give in to the winds and waves of busyness and popularity. Not only will these and other pressures like them blow us off course, but they can potentially smash our boat on the rocks as well.

Good navigators are good because they maintain their focus. The best navigators are able to use the wind and the waves to power their ships in the right direction.

Step No. 3—Invite participation in the Story

Salvation is a "we thing" and not a "me thing." We accomplish God's dream together. We exist to be a community.

You've probably heard someone say, "I don't have to go to church to be a Christian." You may have heard it from a few of your teens. You may be thinking it yourself. Yet when we become participants in the Story, we see that the Bible is clear in its expectations that faith and ministry happen in community. Our relationships are the field on which faith is played out! Today's teens are looking to belong to a people with a cause. The community of faith is the group of people who have the ultimate cause.

Don't make the mistake of underchallenging your teens. The worst thing that we can do is make participation in the Kingdom easier than joining the local YMCA. Instead, we need to make sure that we raise the bar high enough that they see this Story as something worthy of their time and efforts, something worth giving their lives for.

Again, the most effective motivational tool we will employ will be our own lives. We need to regularly ask ourselves, "Is my life an attractive invitation to participate in this Story that continues to be written? Can the teens who are watching me see *how* their faith is found in community and that family membership has both its privileges and its responsibilities?"

We need to call each of our teens to grab an oar. Many times what they will learn about rowing they will find out by watching us with an oar in our hands.

In this book I've outlined the things that should be a priority if our desire is to be a worship-centered youth ministry. I haven't taken the time to list the types of things we need to stop doing. The truth is, if we are doing the things I have mentioned, it will leave little time for other nonessential distractions. I hope you don't see that as bad news. I hope you will be able to see the possibility of involving more of the family of faith in accomplishing the work of youth ministry.

Ours is a most awesome responsibility —to lead young people back to the Story of God.

Is it possible that you are doing some of the things that your teens' parents should be doing? Is it possible that you are doing some of the things that other volunteers should be doing? It is entirely possible, if you insist on doing it all yourself, that you are causing others in your fellowship to miss out on the joy of being involved, and as a result, they are living beneath their privilege as coauthors of the Story. Be careful to do your work, not everyone else's.

You are valued members of the family of faith. You are my fellow youth workers, my fellow Storytellers. Ours is a most awesome responsibility—to lead young people back to the Story of God. Therefore, it is my prayer that God will use for His glory our lives, our mistakes, and our successes as you and I tell and retell the Story to all who will listen. And though we will face wind and waves and the occasional piece of driftwood lurking just beneath the water, our ship must sail on, for our cause is worth every risk.

Reflection Questions

1. As you think about your current ministry, mark on the line below with an *X* where you think you fall as a youth worker.

Activities	Worship-
Director	Centered
	Leader

2. Now, draw on that same line a heart to indicate where you would like to be.

3. In what ways must you change if you are going to become a worship-centered leader?

4. In what ways must your youth ministry change if it is going to become a worship-centered youth ministry?

Appendix A
Biblical Time Line

CREATION

JESUS' SECOND COMING

Appendix B

Sample Letter

The following is a sample letter that I have used to help our parents understand the move from a traditional youth ministry to a worship-centered youth ministry.

Dear First Family and Parents of Our Teens:

As the summer draws to a close, we are already making preparations for what will be a great fall! I hope you and yours have had and are having a great summer!

First I want to give special thanks to all of you who helped us pilot the first-ever Youth Ministry Steering Committee.

MIDDLE SCHOOL PARENTS
Vanette Bell
Larry Hess
Debi Nimz
Debbie Rains
Vicki Snowden

MIDDLE SCHOOL STAFF
Betsy Falley
Chuck Mosley
Sarah Mosley
J. R. O'Hair
Heather Robinson

HIGH SCHOOL PARENTS
Darrell Baskett
Mike Bell
Linda Cannata
Teresa Caraway
Steve Laswell

HIGH SCHOOL STAFF
Aaron Copeland
Brett Dawkins
Jon Middendorf
Brad Moore
Maria Thompson

MIDDLE SCHOOL STUDENTS
Philip Cox
Mike Green
Zach Green
Ryan Martin
Morgan Rains
Bennett Snowden

HIGH SCHOOL STUDENTS
Taylor Caraway
Brooke Hess
Melanie Laswell
Heath Webb
Heather Webb

SHEPHERDS IN RESIDENCE: Jerry and Mary Ann Bell

Thanks for being so faithful! With your help many more activities and initiatives were dreamed and carried out!

This committee recently completed its term, and the new council now needs to be nominated and elected and in place for our first meeting, September 10. Your involvement in this ministry to teens is crucial to its success. Please prayerfully consider the roles you can play in shaping the hearts of the teens who are attending and who will attend OKC First!

Pastor Steve continues to talk to all of us on the pastoral staff about the importance of "team." Have you ever been part of a team? Maybe you were on a basketball team at one time. Maybe you were in a choir; maybe a marching band or an orchestra. Maybe you were on an academic team of some kind, a team that worked together on that big school project.

Maybe you are still on some kind of team. Are you on a school or neighborhood action committee? Are you on a church board or committee? Are you on a booster squad or a parent committee of any kind? Hopefully you have had, at one point or another, some experience in being involved in a team. If you have, and particularly if you have been involved in an effective or successful team, you know the benefit of teamwork, and the resultant good feelings of accomplishment, synergy, ownership, and fulfillment that can be yours as a result of having participated in a real team.

I have had the privilege of working on many of these kinds of teams. I have always enjoyed that "teammate" connection to the people with whom I have shared responsibility, challenges, and success. Right now, your ministry staff is working to foster that good team feeling.

Parents, it is my sincere prayer that together we can find new and better ways to work together as teammates in youth ministry.

On September 10, I would like to meet with the new Youth Ministry Steering Committee that would be comprised of five parents of teens currently involved in our ministry, five members of the youth council, the NYI president, two members of the volunteer youth staff, and the youth pastor. (It is my intention that there would be two steering committees: one for the high school ministry and one for the middle school ministry.)

After the meeting on the 10th, this committee would meet once a month—on the second Sunday of every month, from 4:30 to 6 P.M. in the Caritas Sunday School classroom.

Our meetings would look something like this: a time of prayer, a brief discussion on a philosophy of youth ministry, a time of review (the previous month's activities), and a time of planning and preparation done in smaller committees (see the following page).

These meetings will not be Jon's repackaged youth ministry seminars. They will not be "target practice." Criticism for criticism's sake helps no one. They will not be boring. We will be busy; we'll do more than our share of laughing, and we probably won't finish on time very often. They will not be dinnertimes. Eat a little something before you come, or plan a big shindig after the evening service.

Earlier I mentioned smaller committees. How will the larger committee be divided into the smaller committees? I'm so glad you asked . . .

If you've been listening, you've heard Pastor Steve talk about what he believes to be the five essential practices of the church as seen throughout the Bible and Church history.

Those practices are:
1. The Formation of Christian Community—an embracing of one another as the people of God, and the "practicing" of openness, confession, vulnerability, encouragement, and support—habits that will serve to pull us closer together as we all pull closer to God.

2. Praise—the magnification and glorification of God because of who He is.

3. Witness—the sharing of the good news of and about Christ.

4. Works of Mercy—compassionate ministry; more than "tokenism" or "hit and run" compassion, the intention here is for an ongoing, never-ending commitment to others.

5. Discernment—practice in using the wisdom of God to see through the wisdom of the world.

Our pastor refers to these as practices. But it might help you to think of these five habits as rhythms. A rhythm is regular and ongoing. In the same way, our youth ministry (and our church) will be most healthy when we commit ourselves to these five rhythms. I would like to divide our larger committee into five committees, each committee focusing on one of the above rhythms.

The Christian Community Committee would focus its efforts on the creation of regularly occurring events that would help to form this group of teens toward true community. The Worship Committee would focus its efforts on the creation of regularly occurring events that would help teens see the glory and majesty of God (devotional material, musical events, Sunday School, Wednesday nights). The Witness Committee would focus its efforts on the creation of regularly occurring events that would help our teens (and our church) see the necessity of and the joy in telling the Story of God and His people to those who have yet to hear it. The Works of Mercy Committee would focus its efforts on the creation of regularly occurring events that would help our teens see the necessity of and the joy in liberating people from all kinds of bondage. The Discernment Committee would focus its efforts on the creation of regularly occurring events that would help teens be formed after the image of Christ.

I'm sure that the work of many of these committees would overlap. That's a good thing! Let's take every opportunity to build team! Each month we'll look at the youth calendar just to make sure that we are regularly committed to the essential rhythms. Each committee will work to intertwine parental leadership, youth staff leadership, and youth leadership, so that each facet of our ministry can enjoy the benefit of balance, teamwork, and synergy!

Here's what I need from you. Enclosed you'll find an already stamped postcard. On the card you'll see that you have an opportunity to nominate parents to be parts of the new steering committee. Also included in this packet is a listing of the teens and families that are connected to this ministry. In some sense, this will work like an election. As I receive your responses, I will tabulate the results and contact the people you have nominated. In the event that the person you have chosen declines to participate, I will contact the next person in line to fill that particular position.

Please feel free to vote for yourself! We need willing helpers on this committee. If you are willing and available, don't hesitate to recommend yourself!

If by chance you are willing to be involved, but you are not elected, stay encouraged! If you communicate to me that you are willing to work in a particular area, I will see to it that you have opportunity to help!

Here are a few things to keep in mind:
- I need you to return your responses to me as soon as possible, no later than February 1.
- We are forming both a high school and a middle school council. Make sure that you are high school parents for the high school council, and so on.
- Nominate the people who would be willing to serve.
- Again, please feel free to nominate yourself!
- Try to keep the uniqueness of the each subcommittee in mind when nominating parents.
- The first meeting will be on February 13. The following meetings will take place on the first Sunday of every month, from 5 to 6 P.M. in the Green Activity Center.

I want your input on this thing. If by chance you want to submit your nominations via the web, you can E-mail them to me. The anonymity is lost, but you might find it quicker and easier.

Thank you, in advance, for your help. I want what you want—a balanced, healthy, effective ministry for your teens and for those teens who have yet to find a church to call home.

Your Youth Pastor,
Jon Middendorf

CROSSROADS
-The roads to and from the CROSS

MATTHEW 1 & 2 "God's Dream Becomes a Baby"

LAST WEEK: Nehemiah 9 & 10 The Exiles return to Jerusalem and
rebuild the city and the wall.
—They hear the whole story retold.
—They recommit themselves to the
habits that make relationship with God
possible.
Nehemiah 13 The people of Israel fail again.
The situation seems hopeless.
400 years of SILENCE.

[1]A record of the genealogy of Jesus Christ the son of David, the son of Abraham:

[2]Abraham was the father of Isaac, Isaac the father of Jacob, Jacob the father of Judah and his brothers, [3]Judah the father of Perez and Zerah, whose mother was Tamar, Perez the father of Hezron, Hezron the father of Ram, [4]Ram the father of Amminadab, Amminadab the father of Nahshon, Nahshon the father of Salmon, [5]Salmon the father of Boaz, whose mother was Rahab, Boaz the father of Obed, whose mother was Ruth, Obed the father of Jesse, [6]and Jesse the father of King David.

David was the father of Solomon, whose mother had been Uriah's wife, [7]Solomon the father of Rehoboam, Rehoboam the father of Abijah, Abijah the father of Asa, [8]Asa the father of Jehoshaphat, Jehoshaphat the father of Jehoram, Jehoram the father of Uzziah, [9]Uzziah the father of Jotham, Jotham the father of Ahaz, Ahaz the father of Hezekiah, [10]Hezekiah the father of Manasseh, Manasseh the father of Amon, Amon the father of Josiah, [11]and Josiah the father of Jeconiah and his brothers at the time of the exile to Babylon.

[12]After the exile to Babylon: Jeconiah was the father of Shealtiel, Shealtiel the father of Zerubbabel, [13]Zerubbabel the father of Abiud, Abiud the father of Eliakim, Eliakim the father of Azor, [14]Azor the father of Zadok, Zadok the father of Akim, Akim the father of Eliud, [15]Eliud the father of Eleazar, Eleazar the father of Matthan, Matthan the father of Jacob, [16]and Jacob the father of Joseph, the husband of Mary, of whom was born Jesus, who is called Christ.

So Jesus didn't so much come from ABOVE , but from BEFORE . Jesus
was GOD —He continued to write the STORY of the PEOPLE of
GOD .

KEY PEOPLE AND EVENTS IN THE GENEALOGY OF CHRIST—

1. Abraham (1:2)   Read Genesis 12:2–3. He was the _FATHER_ of God's people.

2. David (1:6)   He was the _HERO_ of God's people, a man after God's own _HEART_.

3. Exile (1:11)   This was the most painful _MEMORY_ of God's people.

4. Tamar (1:3)   She tricked _PEREZ_ into continuing the family tree.

5. Rahab (1:5)   A _PROSTITUTE_ who helped _JOSHUA_ defeat _JERICHO_.

6. Bathsheba (1:16)   She had an _AFFAIR_ with King David. David had her husband _URIAH_ killed. She gave birth to _SOLOMON_, the next King.

Still God's dream is to _HAVE A PEOPLE TO CALL HIS OWN_. He has, He is and He will work to accomplish this dream in and through _REAL PEOPLE_.

The people of Israel had not been able to live as the _PEOPLE_ of God. So, God sent His son into the world, in the form of a _CHILD_, to be an example of _FAITHFUL OBEDIENCE_. In being obedient, in _LIFE_ and _DEATH_, Jesus became the _PATTERN_, the _LIGHT_, and the _POWER_ for us—the new people of God.

Discussion Questions

1. What can we know about God based on what we have heard in this story?

2. What can we know about humankind based on what we have heard in this story?

3. What are God's dreams for us?

NEXT WEEK: "Jesus gets baptized."—Read Matthew 3

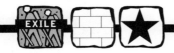

TIME LINE

Appendix D

Sample E-mail Reading List for Youth Devotions

MONDAY

Hi, everyone! Sorry we have missed you over the last couple of days!

Don't forget:

1. Keep your Bibles nearby and do the reading.
2. Feedback helps me a lot.
3. Devotionals will "appear" Monday through Friday afternoons.
4. *Be consistent.* You will see benefits soon enough. If you are not consistent, you will find that it will be harder and harder to start.

NOW FOR TODAY'S DEVOTION

Read Exodus 7:14-24.

Write down your first impressions.

Why would this story be included in this book?

What was the theme of the Book of Exodus?

How does this passage of Scripture fit into the overall theme?

Write down a few words and phrases (at least five things) that you would use to describe Moses based on what you know so far.

Write down a few words and phrases (at least five things) that you would use to describe God based on what you have seen in Exodus so far.

Write down a few words and phrases (at least five things) that you would use to describe Pharaoh based on what you have seen in Exodus so far.

See you soon. When was the last time I told you all how much you mean to this tall, inept white boy with pretty bad hair? Well, that's much too long.

Jon

P.S. If you read this one, you get a Braum's shake on me. Give me the big phone call.

TUESDAY

Hi, everyone!

Don't forget:

1. Keep your Bibles nearby and do the reading.
2. Feedback helps me a lot.
3. Devotionals will "appear" Monday through Friday afternoons.
4. *Be consistent.* You will see benefits soon enough. If you are not consistent, you will find that it will be harder and harder to start.

NOW FOR TODAY'S DEVOTION

Read Exodus 7:25—8:15.
Write down your first impressions.

Frogs in the water? Gross . . .

The magicians could do the same things (see v. 7). Didn't God know they were going to try and do something like this? Why did God let it happen anyway?

Why did Moses keep believing Pharaoh? (v. 10)

Why did Pharaoh's heart harden? (v. 15)

Why would this story be included in this book?

What was the theme of the Book of Exodus?

How does this passage of Scripture fit into the overall theme?

Write down a few words and phrases (at least five things) that you would use to describe Moses based on what you know so far.

Write down a few words and phrases (at least five things) that you would use to describe God based on what you have seen in Exodus so far.

Write down a few words and phrases (at least five things) that you would use to describe Pharaoh based on what you have seen in Exodus so far.

See you soon. When was the last time I told you all how much you mean to this tall, inept white boy with bad hair? Well, that's much too long.

Jon

P.S. If you read this one, you get a Braum's shake on me. Give me a phone call.

WEDNESDAY

Hi, everyone!

Don't forget:

1. Keep your Bibles nearby and do the reading.
2. Feedback helps me a lot.
3. Devotionals will "appear" Monday through Friday afternoons.
4. *Be consistent.* You will see benefits soon enough. If you are not consistent, you will find that it will be harder and harder to start.

NOW FOR TODAY'S DEVOTION

Read Exodus 8:16-32.

Write down your first impressions.

What must it have been like to have gnats everywhere? What would you do?

Why did Moses keep believing Pharaoh? (v. 32)

Why did Pharaoh's heart harden? (v. 32)

Why would this story be included in this book?

What was the theme of the Book of Exodus?

How does this passage of Scripture fit into the overall theme?

Write down a few words and phrases (at least five things) that you would use to describe Moses based on what you know so far.

Write down a few words and phrases (at least five things) that you would use to describe God based on what you have seen in Exodus so far.

Write down a few words and phrases (at least five things) that you would use to describe Pharaoh based on what you have seen in Exodus so far.

See you soon. When was the last time I told you all how much you mean to this tall, inept white boy with bad hair? Well, that's much too long.

Jon

P.S. Devotionals will stop after December 23 and pick up on January 5.

HAPPY HOLIDAYS!

Appendix E

Suggested Reading List

The following books will further your understanding of the issues discussed in this book.

Barna, George. 1995. *Generation NeXt*. Ventura, Calif.: Regal Books.

Bonhoeffer, Dietrich. 1954. *Life Together*. San Francisco: Harper Collins.

Borgman, Dean. 1997. *When Kumbaya Is Not Enough: A Practical Theology for Youth Ministry*. Peabody, Mass.: Hendrickson Publishers.

Brueggemann, Walter. 1993. *Biblical Perspectives on Evangelism*. Nashville: Abingdon Press.

Clapp, Rodney. 1996. *A Peculiar People: The Church as Culture in a Post-Christian Society*. Downers Grove, Ill.: InterVarsity Press.

Dawn, Marva. 1995. *Reaching Out Without Dumbing Down*. Grand Rapids: Eerdmans Publishing Co.

Dean, Kenda Creasy, and Ron Foster. 1998. *The Godbearing Life: The Art of Soul Tending for Youth Ministry*. Nashville: Upper Room Books.

Dulles, Avery. 1987. *Models of the Church*. New York: Doubleday.

Lodahl, Michael. 1994. *The Story of God*. Kansas City: Beacon Hill Press of Kansas City.

Long, Jimmy. 1997. *Generating Hope: A Strategy for Reaching the Postmodern Generation*. Downers Grove, Ill.: InterVarsity Press.

Murphy, Nancey. 1996. *Beyond Liberalism and Fundamentalism: How Modern and Postmodern Philosophy Set the Theological Agenda*. Valley Forge, Pa.: Trinity Press International.

Robbins, Duffy. 1996. *The Ministry of Nurture: How to Build Real-Life Faith into Your Kids*. Grand Rapids: Zondervan.

Tapscott, Don. 1997. *Growing Up Digital: The Rise of the Net Generation*. New York: McGraw-Hill.

Ward, Pete. 1999. *God at the Mall: Youth Ministry That Meets Kids Where They're At*. Peabody, Mass.: Hendrickson.

Reference List

Barna, George. 1995. *Generation NeXt*. Ventura, Calif.: Regal Books.

Boerner, Michael. 1997. *Video Illustration Project*. Boise, Idaho: Mission Media.

Campolo, Tony. "Christianity for Alienated Teenagers, *Youthworker Journal* (summer 1991).

Clapp, Rodney. 1996. *A Peculiar People: The Church as Culture in a Post-Christian Society*. Downers Grove, Ill.: InterVarsity Press.

Dawn, Marva. 1995. *Reaching Out Without Dumbing Down*. Grand Rapids: Eerdmans Publishing Co.

Dale, Edgar. 1969. *Audio-Visual Methods in Teaching*. New York: Holt, Rinehart, and Winston, Inc.

Fields, Doug, et al. 1996. *Spontaneous Melodramas*. Grand Rapids: Zondervan.

Harrison, Everett F. 1976. *Romans, 1 Corinthians, 2 Corinthians, Galatians*. Vol. 10 of *The Expositor's Bible Commentary*, ed. Frank E. Gaebelein. Grand Rapids: Zondervan.

"ICR Teen Excel Survey." *USA Today*, August 17, 1998.

Clark, Chap. "The Needs of the Class of 2004," *Ivy Jungle*. Vol. 7, summer 1999.

Lodahl, Michael. 1994. *The Story of God*. Kansas City: Beacon Hill Press of Kansas City.

Long, Jimmy. 1997. *Generating Hope*. Downers Grove, Ill.: InterVarsity Press.

McDowell, Josh, and Bob Hostetler. 1994. *Right from Wrong: What You Need to Know to Help Youth Make Right Choices*. Dallas: Word Publishing.

Nouwen, Henri. 1972. *The Wounded Healer*. New York: Image Books.

Nouwen, Henri, et al. 1982. *Compassion: A Reflection on the Christian Life*. New York: Image Books.

Rainer, Thom S. 1997. *The Bridger Generation*. Nashville: Broadman and Holman Publishers.

Robbins, Duffy. 1996. *The Ministry of Nurture: How to Build Real-Life Faith into Your Kids*. Grand Rapids: Zondervan.

Stott, John. 1992. *The Contemporary Christian: Applying God's Word to Today's World*. Downers Grove, Ill.: InterVarsity Press.

Strauss, William, and Neil Howe. 1997. *The Fourth Turning*. New York: Broadway Books.

Tapscott, Don. 1997. *Growing Up Digital: The Rise of the Net Generation*. New York: McGraw-Hill.